Norf
Ghosts
and
Legends

Polly Howat

COUNTRYSIDE BOOKS

NEWBURY, BERKSHIRE

First Published 1993
© Polly Howat 1993

COUNTRYSIDE BOOKS
3 Catherine Road
Newbury, Berkshire

ISBN 1 85306 257 X

Produced through MRM Associates Ltd., Reading
Printed in England

For David Mould
– with my best wishes

Introduction

Folklore is an important subject. It not only allows us an insight into the traditions of our forefathers, but also helps us to identify with them and with our landscape. People still claim to encounter the supernatural and have strange, inexplicable experiences. Others have wonderful family stories and memories, which they have shared generously with me.

Happily the subject is not dead. Many still enjoy both the old tales and the modern ones which are being passed on in pubs, schools, workplaces and dining rooms. Instead of 'headless horsemen' our modern anxieties are manifested in 'urban myths and legends'.

Much of our late 20th century anguish is evident in these semi-plausible stories. They highlight our occasional need to come to terms with fear and mistrust for much the same reason as our traditional legends evolved. Although less rich than many of the old localised subjects, the modern ones still play an important part in current folk culture.

This book concentrates mainly on the county's traditional ghosts and legends, with some recent updates. It is written for all age groups since I am aware that children, the storytellers of the future, are also interested in the subject. Some of the tales will be well known, others less so and some will be new to you.

I have also included a glossary of Norfolk words to add to your enjoyment. This wonderful dialect could soon be a thing of the past, thanks to standard English and our fast-moving, cosmopolitan lifestyles. Should this happen, it will be a tremendous loss.

Polly Howat
Wisbech
1993

ASHWELLTHORPE

The Magic Oak Tree

THE present Ashwellthorpe Hall is a Tudor-style building dating from 1831, standing at the edge of the village, four and a half miles south-east of Wymondham. The family of Knyvet, or Knevet, lived an Ashwellthorpe in the 16th and 17th centuries. The old hall was built by Sir Thomas Knyvet the elder. He was renowned for his hospitality and good nature and was knighted by Elizabeth I during her state journey through Norfolk in 1578.

According to a ballad printed by Blomefield in 1769, under the title *The Ballad of Ashwell-Thorp, made in Sir Thomas Knevet's Time*, a mysterious traveller one day offered to perform an amazing trick, which almost ruined the Norfolk knight's Christmas party.

The stranger came from London and was travelling around Norfolk for his own amusement. It was Christmas Eve when he arrived at Ashwellthorpe Hall, where Sir Thomas was holding a festive revel for his many friends. The traveller was not begging for food and money, the usual quest of casual callers. In fact he had something to offer the great man – a fabulous trick. Hypnotism is a possible explanation for what is then said to have occurred.

Sir Thomas was intrigued and welcomed him into his home, for a little magic would add to the enjoyment of his party. The traveller was escorted into the great hall. He produced from his pocket what he claimed to be a magic acorn which could immediately grow into a large tree. It was handed to the bemused assembly for inspection and all agreed that it certainly looked real enough. The acorn was then placed in the middle of the room and before his audience had time to finish their wine, a massive oak tree sprang up and filled the place. It was a splendid, mature specimen, with huge branches groaning under the weight of the ripened black and brown acorns which bounced like hailstones onto the floor. Servants were ordered to gather them up and cart them off to the pigsties.

5

By now it was getting late and time for supper. The porkers might have been content with their unexpected meal, but the guests were decidedly hungry. However, the tree was so big there was no place to set the table, let alone dance afterwards. This did not bother the traveller. He had promised them a large tree and a large tree was what they got! Eventually Sir Thomas called for two of his strongest men to fell the oak, which was no longer a novelty. Its begetter watched the woodcutters hard at work.

'I'll tell you here no lye,
The chips then there did flye,
Buzzing about like flyes,
That men were forced to ward,
Their faces well to guard,
For fear they sh'd lose their eyes.'

At last the almost impossible task was accomplished and the tree crashed to the ground, but it was too heavy to move. Everyone except the traveller lent a hand to try to shift the dead weight, but it was no good. It would not budge one inch.

The traveller found it all very funny and teased them for their feebleness. He would perform another trick to prove his point. Hey presto! Two tiny, fluffy goslings waddled in, picked up the oak in their beaks and carried it out of the door as if it were no heavier than a worm.

Blomefield ends his ballad by saying.

'This story is true,
Which I have told you . . .'

Legend says that about the time of this tale there was a manor house at Huntingfield, Suffolk which had a great forest of trees growing within it. We are not told how they got there. Perhaps the owner received the same mysterious traveller who knocked on Sir Thomas's door.

Presumably Sir Thomas Knyvet and his guests dined out on this oak tree trick for many years, even though there was not one splinter of proof that it had ever sprung to life in Ashwellthorpe Hall. For as soon as the little geese rested it on the lawn, it wasted away so quickly that 'not one chip could then be found' and doubtless the pigs had eaten all its fruit.

AYLMERTON

The Shrieking Pits

THE whole area around Aylmerton and West Runton Heath is dotted with shallow, circular iron workings that date from about AD 850–1100. They were quarries for the extraction of iron nodules from glacial sand; pieces of slag from the primitive smelting furnaces may be found in the walls of local Saxon churches. The legend of the Shrieking Pits originates from this ancient landscape.

At Aylmerton some depressions in a field on the western side of the road past St John's church and just before the iron railings, enjoy a sinister reputation. The place is said to be haunted by a distraught and deathly-pale woman. She has long floating hair and wears an ankle-length white dress. The apparition roams from one hole to another, peering into each. When she fails to find what she is seeking, she wrings her hands with anguish and lets out a terrible shriek. It echoes most dreadfully around the neighbourhood, compelling people to stay within the safety of their homes. Then the ghostly creature moves slowly on and gazes down into the next 'grave', the moonlight adding to her pallor.

Nothing untoward seems to have occurred for many years, yet this inquisitive spectre with the death-rattling voice remains an important part of local folklore. They say she is hunting for the body of her baby who was buried in one of these hollows by her wicked husband a long time ago. Sadly she does not know in which, hence her eternal searching. The legend continues that not only did the man kill his own child, but he went on to murder his wife when half-crazed with jealousy. What caused his outrageous passion and whether or not he met his come-uppance has been lost with time.

Over the centuries these industrial relics of Saxon quarrying have become wide open to supernatural interpretation, for inexplicable holes were often regarded with fear and super-stition. If not the Devil or some unhallowed phenomenon, who could have put them there and why? Even now, when we know the history of the area, a windy moonlit night could well play tricks on someone taking a solitary walk past the field at that certain hour which throws up fears from long ago. It is such primitive emotions which help prevent the old traditions from completely fading away.

BACTON

The True Cross

ON a clear night visitors to Bacton, eleven miles south-east of Cromer, could be forgiven for thinking they were in fairy land, such are the myriad twinkling lights surrounding the huge North Sea Gas terminal. What a contrast it is, compared with the stark welcome which must have greeted the hordes of pilgrims who once made their way to Bromholm Priory nearby.

It was founded in 1113 by William de Glandeville as a cell for the Cluniac monks at Castle Acre Priory. Its ruins today stand on private land at the top of Abbey Street, but can be easily seen from the road. The place was poor and humble, until a Norfolk priest named Hugh, who had been a chaplain to the Emperor Baldwin of Constantinople, paid a visit in the 13th century. He brought with him what he claimed was a piece of the True Cross of Calvary, stained with the Blood of Christ. This was an incredibly rare and valuable relic, or Holy Rood.

It is said that Hugh of Norfolk had stolen this along with other divine relics after the death of the previous owner – the Emperor himself! The great man had always carried this wondrous Holy Rood when he went into battle. One day he forgot his talisman. He was slain and his army defeated. Crafty Hugh seized his chance and made off with the sacred booty. He had travelled across Europe offering this and other mementos for sale, but his asking price for the relics of the True Cross was too high, even for the wealthiest monasteries.

When most of his money was used up and times were getting hard for the wandering monk, he arrived at the impoverished Bromholm Priory. Worn out from journeying so far, the priest desperately wanted to return to his roots and his only wish was to take refuge in a Norfolk monastery. By now his one remaining treasure was less of monetary value than a means of satisfying this need. Eventually a deal was struck with the abbot of Bromholm, who received the precious relic free of charge in return for Hugh's unconditional admittance into his community.

Immediately the fortunes of this almost unknown religious house changed. Many miracles were claimed by the touching of the ancient pieces of wood; 39 people were brought back from the dead, 19 blind people had their eyesight restored. Lepers were cured of their disease. The list of wonders was long and the pieces of the True Cross brought great wealth and fame to Bromholm. For a time it even rivalled Walsingham as a centre of pilgrimage, and was endowed with royal privileges.

'By the Holy Rood of Bromholm' became a binding medieval oath. In the literature of that time, Piers Plowman's tradesman beseeched it to bring him out of debt, while Chaucer's miller's daughter also called on the cross to help her.

Bromholm enjoyed its great prosperity until 1424, when a visitor deliberately threw the relic into the fire. As the True Cross turned to ashes, so did the popularity of this famous priory. There was nothing left to attract the pilgrims and their large financial offerings. No more miracles. Nothing but the established routine of monastic life. Bromholm quickly reverted to its former anonymity, and eventually shared the fate of other monastic houses with dissolution in 1536.

This was the end of the priory, whose fame and prosperity came from a holy artefact and died with its destruction. The stone ruins give no hint of the wonders which drew such crowds – life from death, sight from blindness and all those other miracles performed not far from the lap of the cold North Sea.

The Long Coastguardsman

THE three mile coastal path linking Bacton with Mundesley is said to be the old haunt of a certain invisible spectre known as the 'Long Coastguardsman'. He has not made his presence known for a long time, but according to tradition he always set out from Bacton to Mundesley at the stroke of midnight on stormy, moonless nights.

Although never seen, he sang and shouted at the top of his voice when gales lashed at this north-east Norfolk coast. Then he laughed terrifyingly when there was a lull in the wind. Sometimes his loud cries for help echoed around this dreadful route, but people were always too scared to save him.

Who would have gone out in that vile weather at the dead of night to help the invisible 'Long Coastguardsman', who shrieked like a storm force ten! His previous human identity is unknown. Maybe he was indeed a tall coastguard, who drowned at sea in a terrible storm, or perhaps met with a fatal accident on that path. The storm must have reminded the fishing communities of their vulnerability to the elements: travellers battered and bent almost double, picking their way through the dark night; lanterns flickering horrid shadows, or suddenly going out; the eerie whistling wind forcing its way through tightly shut windows and doors. Indeed, who would willingly leave their shelter today, to walk the path from Bacton to Mundesley in a raging gale.

BAWBURGH

St Walstan

THE shrine of St Walstan, once housed in the parish church of St Mary and St Walstan, was an ancient centre of pilgrimage. Nearby, a well stands in a tranquil setting, a few hundred yards down the lane from the church. It is said that its water spouted spontaneously from the ground when his dead body found its final resting place.

This popular saint was born at Bawburgh, some four miles west of Norwich, between AD 960 and AD 970. His father, Benedict, is believed to have been related to King Edmund Ironside. His mother was possibly St Blide, who is thought to be buried at St Mary's at Martham and to whom the south aisle altar is dedicated.

Despite his noble parentage, this deeply religious boy left home at the age of twelve to live a life of poverty. He became a labourer on a farm at Taverham, seven miles north of Bawburgh, but was no ordinary farm-hand. Walstan had no need of possessions. Everything he owned was given to the poor, including his food, shoes and meagre wages. Once when his mistress told him off for his foolishness, she found him barefoot, loading a cart with thorns yet totally unscathed.

His master and his wife were childless and offered to make him their heir, but were refused. The good man lived in austerity for 30 years, healing people and animals through his prayers and ministration. However, in time he did accumulate three possessions. God had revealed Himself in a dream and announced the farmer would offer him two oxen and a cart, which he was to accept.

In his final years Walstan had many visions and learned the reason why the Lord had commanded his acceptance of the farmer's gifts. Walstan instructed his master that when he died, his body was to be placed on the cart and pulled by the oxen. The animals were to be permitted to roam freely and would determine where he was to be buried.

His last dream foretold his death. On his final morning, 30th May 1016, he received Holy Communion out in the fields where he had worked for most of his life. A spring gushed up to mark the place. This could still be seen within memory in an orchard below St Edmund's church at Taverham. As death approached, Walstan prayed that any farm labourer who came to his grave would be cured of ill health, and cattle freed from the murrain. Then he died and a white dove flew from his mouth.

The farmer honoured this holy man's wishes and placed his corpse on the cart. The two oxen were hitched up. They meandered off and in time rested a while in Costessey Wood.

Another spring bubbled out of the ground. Their last stop was in a meadow below Bawburgh church. More miraculous water burst forth, to be known as St Walstan's Well, once famous for curing both humans and animals. His body rested here before burial in the church.

Later Walstan's remains were moved to a specially built transept chapel on the north side of the church and a shrine built over his tomb. Miracles of healing occurred and this became the goal of countless pilgrims. They travelled from all over Britain and the Continent to worship at this place. Great wealth came with them and in 1310 the church was rebuilt with a shrine chapel to accommodate the remains of the saint and the needs of the travellers. At the Reformation the holy relics were taken away and burned. Now only the outlines of the shrine chapel to the north-east of the nave are visible.

St Walstan is not forgotten, for pilgrims of all denominations continue to celebrate his day on 30th May. The well, which is accessible to the public, is an ideal place for private meditation. It is a constant reminder of the man who worked long and hard in the fields and became a patron saint of agriculture.

BINHAM

The Fiddler and his Dog

FIDDLER'S HILL is a scheduled ancient monument and plays an important role in this story. It is also a very good example of a round barrow or burial mound, dating from the early Bronze Age, about 2000–1400 BC. Although there are over 200 similar mounds in Norfolk, few are as impressive as this one, which has never been excavated. The version of the legend which follows is more common than that which appears on the notice board at the site.

Long ago an adventurous fiddler was alleged to have been spirited away at this point. It was during his exploration of a much feared and disused passage, reputed to link the Benedictine priory at Binham with Little Walsingham. It was said to be haunted by a 'Black Monk', but perhaps even this spectre found the tunnel too intimidating. He was claimed to haunt its length above ground on moonless nights!

The legend continues that one day a brave fiddler and his dog strolled into the village. Traditional fears held no menace for him, for he announced that he and his dog were going to explore the passage. The villagers could follow him above ground, if they dared, and he would play his fiddle to mark his progress.

A sizeable crowd was said to have gathered at the entrance to the tunnel at Binham priory, doubtless anxious to witness an over-confident stranger making an idiot of himself. This tempting possibility must have outweighed their fear of bumping into the Black Monk. They wished the adventurer good luck and he and his dog set off on their daring expedition. His followers walked to the strains of his music, and all appeared to be well. However, when the musician got to what is now called Fiddler's Hill, where the present unclassified Binham road off the B1105 meets with the Wighton road, the music stopped abruptly.

The crowd called down to him, but there was no response. A long time later the little dog appeared with his tail between his legs, 'a-shiverin' as if he wor mortal skeered'. Still there was no sign of the fiddler. Eventually the onlookers decided the Black Monk must have gone down and carted the foolish man off! Nobody came forward to investigate, so they went home and presumably the animal wandered off by itself.

They say that later that night a violent storm broke and the following morning the passage entrance was obliterated. The place where the fiddler was lost became known as 'Fiddler's Hill', but he was gone forever.

BIRCHAM NEWTON

Air Force Ghosts

NO wonder so many Air Force stations are said to be haunted. Consider the numerous men in their prime who never returned from their wartime sorties. Think of the tension and anguish that must be almost embedded in the bricks.

The old RAF station at Bircham Newton, some 13 miles north-east of King's Lynn, is no exception. It was originally built in 1916 for the Royal Flying Corps and rebuilt in 1929 with the present buildings. It closed in 1960 and seven years later was taken over by the Construction Industry Training Board. Parts of the camp are said to be haunted, especially one of the squash courts. This is the exceptionally cold one near the old officers' mess. According to one clairvoyant, it contains the spirits of three airmen who were shot down close to St Mary's parish church in 1940.

In August 1970 a film unit moved onto the CITB camp to shoot a management training film. On Friday, 17th December 1971 the *Lynn News & Advertiser* printed a report about a bizarre encounter which befell one of the crew. It was truly a 'haunting experience'.

The assistant soundman, Kevin Garry, decided that although no-one else was interested, he wanted to play squash. He locked himself into a court, which by chance was the infamously cold one, for a solo knock-up. After a while he heard footsteps coming up the stairs which led to the viewing gallery. This was followed by a great sigh. Mr Garry turned round and saw the ghostly figure of an RAF serviceman watching him. The apparition was dressed in full flying kit and he stared at it for several seconds until it vanished into thin air. Then he picked up his belongings and ran terrified from the court and told his colleagues.

It was decided to place a tape recorder in the squash court that night, for proof of any further supernatural activity. The machine would be left playing for one hour. The door was locked, and there was no way in which anyone could get in and tamper with things.

According to Denny Denshaw, another technician, the sounds on the tape were incredible. There were sounds like a person dragging metal objects across the floor, but there was no metal in the place and the floors were wooden. There was also the distinct whine of old aircraft engines taking off and at one point, muffled conversation.

The crew left after two weeks of filming and Mr Denshaw sent the tape to the BBC Jack de Manio programme. It was played over the air one morning. Apparently dogs and cats all over the country went mad as they heard the strange noises coming from their owners' radios. This prompted scores of listeners to write in telling how their pets were affected.

During the week of this 1971 press report, a clairvoyant and medium were called into Bircham to try to solve the mystery of the squash court. The latter detected what he called 'depressed spirits', and the clairvoyant was able to establish contact with them. They said their names were Dusty, Gerry and Pat. The medium then ordered them to go away and not hang on to the earthly world. They did – for a time. The continued activity of the three ghostly airmen still makes the adrenalin flow for those who witness their presence. From time to time they also attract attention from psychic researchers. And why do these spirits choose to hang around the squash court? According to their old friends, they were 'squash mad'!

Dusty, Gerry and Pat are not, however, the sole haunters of Bircham. It is said that a serviceman called Wiley, who committed suicide during the Second World War, makes himself known from time to time.

There is also at least one other. Not so long ago I was speaking to a Fenman about an item for another book. We got onto the subject of ghosts. Did he believe in them? 'Most certainly!' he replied. There was a long pause. He asked if I knew the old Air Force station at Bircham Newton. I nodded. He looked a bit embarrassed. The supernatural is obviously a bit of a ticklish subject.

He had been based there during the Second World War. More silence. He said that I would probably not believe what he was going to tell me, but it was true. Some years ago he had gone back to take a look at the place. Daft as it might sound, he had seen his best mate, a pilot, who had been shot down in action.

There he was, striding out across the camp in his flying gear, just as he had done on that fatal night in 1941.

The old man looked me straight in the eye. He had seen the poor chap in broad daylight. There were no other people or planes. Just his friend, looking straight ahead, going to meet his death. It felt as if time had slipped back 50 years. There was that indescribable touch of war in the air. Tension. Nerves on edge. Death. Ask any serviceman or woman.

The strange thing is, at least for me, the sight of the apparition did not scare him, in fact he said it had the reverse effect. He felt honoured to have seen it and I had to believe his sincerity.

BLACKNOCK

The Screaming Cockler

BLACKNOCK is a mud bank with a terrible tale. It lies more than a mile out to sea off the Stiffkey Salt Marshes, on the north-west coast between High Sand and Stone Mell Creeks. A dangerous place, covered with sea grass. They say it is good for gathering the famous blue-shelled 'Stewkey Blue' cockles, but best avoided unless you know the lie of the land. Keep well away.

The tide races hard and fast over Blacknock, but it never scared those near-Amazonian women cocklers from Stiffkey, whose heyday finished with the Second World War. They knew the sea and did not fear that patch of mud. It took more than that to scare those brave, tough women with reddened faces, patterned by the wind. Dressed in pieces of sacking for warmth and to keep out the wet, strong as men, they shrugged off discomfort and went uncomplaining about their work, raking, netting and collecting the shellfish, their fat rear ends facing the sky. Then, bent almost double, they carried their bulging sacks long distances over sand and marshes, if there was no donkey or bicycle to ease the load.

You had to be tough to be a Stiffkey cockler and it took a lot to make one cry. But cry one did, when caught by the fog out on Blacknock, in the early 19th century. She was out alone when the thick grey blanket descended and prevented her finding the familiar route to the shore. She screamed and cried for help, aware of the tide which had yet to turn. She screamed and yelled, swore and cursed.

The crews on the fishing boats anchored along the coast could hear her from that long distance, shouting through the fog, mad with rage, if not fear. They say the Stiffkey women had loud, booming voices. They had to, if they wanted to converse when working. This one screeched for a pitifully long time, but the fishermen were powerless to help. The incoming tide brought silence. The next day the fog lifted and they found her, drowned on Blacknock.

And for many, many years people said that on some foggy nights they could still hear the screams of the 'Blacknock Woman', calling and begging, screaming and cussing, for the help that never came.

BLAKENEY

The Fiddler and his Cat

BLAKENEY, a port and fishmarket since the Middle Ages, has a wonderful mixture of mud-flats, dunes, saltings, marshes, creeks, open sea and a natural harbour which is protected from the sea by Blakeney Point.

You will see the carving of a man with a white cat walking beside him, on the village sign which stands beside the quay. According to legend, he was a brave and adventurous fiddler, lost forever when attempting to explore a disused system of underground passages. By tradition these linked the three principal buildings in the Blakeney neighbourhood, the Friary, the Guildhall and Wiveton Hall, situated about three quarters of a mile by road north-east of Blakeney church.

These reputed passages would have been roughly two miles long, with half their distance under wet land. The long-forgotten Carmelite Friary stood out on the marshes, close to the mouth of the river Glaven. The barely visible stone remains of its small church are on a rise in the corner of the field where the Norfolk Coastal Path veers round to Cley. It was here that vessels going out to sea were blessed. Mariners and fishermen put thank-offerings into an iron box fixed to the outside of the building, for a successful voyage and a safe return to port.

The friary passage would presumably have joined that from Wiveton Hall and then entered the Guildhall. This 14th century building, with its well-preserved vaulted undercroft, is believed to be the remains of a merchant's house. The undercroft was used as a store for his merchandise. Now owned by English Heritage, it is open to the public and is tucked alongside St Nicholas's church hall.

Doubtless everyone feared this underground network, for when a visiting fiddler announced that he was going to explore it, just for fun, the news travelled fast. Excitement was in the air as a large crowd assembled to watch him and his companion cat go underground at the Guildhall end. The musician promised to play his fiddle all the time he was down there, in order that his progress could be charted from above. The Mayor and Corporation appointed themselves the task of following the music and the man and his pet entered the mysterious, pitch black passage.

True to his word, his jolly sounds filtered up through the ground, which pleased the Mayor and his men who followed the invisible adventurer at a dignified speed. But in time the music grew fainter, until it was heard no more. The hours passed. The official entourage, now joined by most of the citizens of Blakeney, waited patiently. Still there was no reassuring music.

No-one had the courage to search for the poor explorers, who were left to their fate probably somewhere under the marshes. Those who had wished them luck a few hours before, went home to the safety of their beds and the fiddler and his cat were never seen again, except on the wooden sign on Blakeney Quay.

BLICKLING

The Ghosts of Anne and Thomas Boleyn

BLICKLING HALL was once the home of Sir Thomas Boleyn and his daughter Anne, the second wife of Henry VIII and mother of Elizabeth I. Now the property of the National Trust, it is two miles north-west of Aylsham on the B1354.

According to tradition it is haunted by these two members of the wealthy Boleyn family, known as the 'Blickling Ghosts'. Anne materialises each May on the anniversary of her execution. She rides up the hall's straight approach, seated in a black carriage drawn by four headless horses. The coachman is also headless, like his passenger. She cradles hers in her arms, not caring about the blood which drips onto her pristine white dress.

The coach vanishes when it reaches the front entrance. Anne then glides into the hall and walks along its corridors, only the rustle of her skirts revealing her presence.

For some unknown reason, her father, Sir Thomas, has a yearly penance to perform for a thousand years from his death. He drives a coach drawn by four headless horses over a circuit of twelve bridges in Norfolk. These include Aylsham, Burgh, Buxton, Coltishall, Meyton, Oxnead and Wroxham. Like his daughter, he too carries his head under his arm, but his gushes flames from its mouth.

John Glyde states in his *Norfolk Garland*, compiled in the 19th century:

'Few rustics are hardy enough to be found loitering on or near those bridges on that night and the man who spoke of that belief says that he was on one occasion hailed by this fiendish apparition, and asked to open a gate, but "he warn't sich a fool as to turn his head; and well a' didn't, for Sir Thomas passed him full gallop like", and he heard a voice which told him that he (Sir Thomas) had no power to hurt such as turned a deaf ear to his requests, but that had he stopped he would have carried him off.'

The Boleyns do not seem to have made an appearance at Blickling for many years, neither have they been sighted at any of their numerous other Norfolk 'haunts'.

BLOFIELD

A Ghostly Duel

AS at Blickling, the hapless Anne Boleyn and her father Sir Thomas play their role in this ghostly tale. According to legend this also involves Sir Thomas Paston, the head of one of the county's leading families and courtier to Henry VIII.

The story says that when Lady Anne Boleyn married Henry VIII, Sir Thomas Paston became obsessively jealous over the honours and privileges bestowed on her family. The Pastons and the Boleyns soon became deadly enemies. When the king decided to rid himself of Anne, he involved Paston in his treachery. He was ordered to prove her guilty of the various misdemeanours of which she was charged, which included incest with her brother. The plan worked.

After the queen's execution, her father, Sir Thomas Boleyn, is said to have challenged Sir Thomas Paston to a duel. They met on the path leading from Blofield church to St Michael's at Braydeston, six miles east of Norwich. The courtiers escaped unscathed, but Paston's servants were killed when their carriage overturned in a stream.

The scene is re-enacted on the anniversary of the tragedy. Lady Anne watches from the safety of her phantom carriage. She is dressed in black velvet, accompanied by four servants and eight headless horses. The animals each have a blue flame flaring from their necks, whilst the two knights do battle with no ordinary weapons. Theirs are swords of fire! When one man is overcome, the ground opens up and receives him. At the same time the other vanishes.

The battle has not taken place for many years. However, the

citizens of Blofield and Braydeston must have given their church path a wide berth in the days when such things were believed. The ghostly duel between the two mighty Sir Thomases was best fought in private.

BRECKLES

Who Killed George Mace?

BRECKLES HALL was built in the 13th century and stands on the edge of Breckland, some eight miles north-east of Thetford, off the A1075.

There are several versions of this tale, which is based around the hall. It concerns the mysterious death of a local villain called George Mace, described as a sly, satanic woman-hater, highway robber and poacher. He always had plenty of money and wore a velvet jacket. They say he won it off a gamekeeper, at a skittles match. Mace hated gamekeepers more than anything else and the coat was a badge of 'divine justice'.

The incident is believed to have happened one Christmas in the early 19th century. Times were hard for the owner of Breckles Hall, Squire Taylor, who was rumoured to be so poor he had barely enough money to feed himself. He could not afford one ancient servant to service his near-derelict home. Locals reckoned that even the rats, who had the free run of the place, were cold.

Mace was the leader of a gang of four poachers. As usual they met on that particular night in a pub in Hockham before going out shooting pheasants. Mace was elected look-out man. Their plan was to meet up at the hall at a certain time, when they would divide their spoils. They would be quite safe because the squire was away and the place would be empty. The men finished their beer and went about their illegal work, confident of success. Later they proceeded to Breckles Hall, to find Mace already standing in the porch.

However, before they could greet him a rumbling noise was heard. It was a brightly lit coach racing up the long straight drive. The poachers dived for cover, but Mace seemed unaware of what was happening. Suddenly the house sprang into light, its stained-glass windows casting weird patterns on the frosty ground. Inside, the frightened poachers could see lords and ladies dressed in old-fashioned clothes, dancing to music – but there was no sound.

The coach stopped at the front door. Its steps were lowered. The carriage door opened and out stepped a woman whom the poachers claimed had 'eyes of death'. She stood stock still, staring long and hard at George Mace, who with one frightful scream fell at her feet. The apparition returned to the coach and slammed the door. The moon went behind a cloud and the phantom coach vanished in the dark.

The thieves ran away, scared out of their wits, not daring to get anywhere near the man on the ground. The next morning he was found lying dead at the front door of Breckles Hall. There was not a mark on his body, but fear was still stamped upon his glassy, staring eyes. They said the Devil must have claimed his own, sending a messenger from hell to steal the soul of that sinner.

The hall was still a sinister building when Dr Augustus Jessop, the Norfolk antiquarian, and witness of the Mannington Hall ghost, paid a visit later in the 19th century. He described it as being 'a house which, for 300 years, no owner seems to have been able to hand down to a grandson of his own . . . it was a house in which two of its owners are said to have committed suicide . . .'

It is now restored to a fine residence, standing in open country. Its long straight approach gives no hint of phantom coaches or the fate of one of the biggest scoundrels of his time.

CAISTER CASTLE

Sir John Fastolf

SIR JOHN FASTOLF (1380–1459) once owned Blickling Hall, and is said to have founded Caister Castle in an original way. During the battle of Agincourt in 1415, Sir John captured the Duc d'Alençon and brought him to England. As a ransom for his own release, the prisoner was made to build his captor a castle at Caister, similar to his own in France. Its ruins stand one mile west of Caister-on-Sea, by a minor road off the A1064.

Shakespeare is reputed to have used Sir John Fastolf for the creation of his character 'Sir John Falstaff'. However, as often pointed out by those who have studied the matter, including Joseph Pennell, author of *Highways and Byways of East Anglia*, published in 1914, the characters could not be more different:

> 'Like an old Norfolk historian, I am indignant that this truly great and eminent character has, by a quibble of the name, been, by hypercritics, supposed the Sir John Falstaff which our immortal bard Shakespeare has exhibited in the various characters of an old, humorous, vapouring, cowardly, lewd, lying and necessitous debauchee, who was constantly lounging about Prince Henry's court.'

However, this brave fighter and fair commander was said to have had a quick temper. He also had a certain reluctance to open his purse, and a foul tongue when the occasion arose. At one time he was in charge of a convoy of 1,200 men, taking a large provision of food to the English troops at war with France. They were attacked by 3,000 of the enemy. Sir John managed not only to save the provisions, but also gave the French a good thrashing. This incident became known as the 'Battle of the Herrings', the salted fish being the major part of the food supply. Doubtless its source was Great Yarmouth.

Sir John Fastolf endowed both Cambridge and Oxford universities and died in his eightieth year at Magdalen College, Oxford, when it was ordained that:

'The monks should sing and the bells should toll,
All for the weale of Fastolff's soul.'

He was buried in a chapel built by himself at the north side of the abbey church of St Benet's-at-Holme, alongside the river Bure.

The castle grounds at Caister are said to be haunted by Anne Boleyn. She arrives on the anniversary of her death, riding in her coach drawn by four headless horses driven by a headless coachman. Her ghost must be the busiest in Norfolk!

Sir John would be amazed if he could see his beloved castle today. A veteran and vintage car museum stands alongside its ruins, plus the Festival of Britain Tree Walks removed from Battersea Park after the Festival of Britain. All are open daily except Saturdays, from mid May to the end of September.

CAISTER-ON-SEA

The Maiden's Tomb

UNTIL its removal in 1896, there was a so-called 'tomb' on top of the tower of the church of the Holy Trinity with St Edmund, which stands in Norwich Road. Before Caister grew into what is now almost a suburb of Great Yarmouth, this 'tomb' would have been visible from the sea.

A legend arose locally to account for this unusual piece of architecture. A certain young local girl, it was said, died from grief following the drowning of her sweetheart. He was returning from a long sea voyage when his ship was wrecked on Scroby Sand, not far from the coast. The girl went into an immediate decline and as she lay on her death bed, made a strange request. She asked that her corpse be entombed on the tower top of the church and placed under a pyramid. This was to be raised high enough to serve as a sea mark in this town, which is famous for its brave lifeboatmen.

24

In fact her legendary 'resting place' was no more than the apex of the tiled roof of the tower, which projected over the battlements. However, for many years it was known as 'The Maiden's Tomb'. It was a symbol of true love and told sailors that they were close to Caister-on-Sea and the safety of its shores.

CASTLE RISING

The She-wolf of France

ACCORDING to tradition, Castle Rising was once a thriving seaport, before it was robbed of its access to the Wash by the silting up of the river Babingley. An ancient rhyme tells us that:

> 'Rising was a seaport town,
> When Lynn was but a marsh;
> Now Lynn it is a seaport town,
> And Rising fares the worse!'

Queen Isabella did not fare too well either, during her reputed 'imprisonment' in Castle Rising castle in the 14th century. This impressive part-ruinous building dominates the village, which lies some four miles from the coast and five miles north-east of King's Lynn.

According to the story Isabella, wife of Edward II, and popularly known as 'The She-wolf of France', was incarcerated in the castle for 27 years. She has been described as being both the most beautiful and the most depraved woman of her time. One of her crimes was the role of principal accomplice in both the deposition and the murder in 1327 of her weak husband. Shortly after his death and the execution of her lover Roger Mortimer, her son, Edward III, had her imprisoned at Castle Rising for treachery. He was said to have ordered her 'to be confined in a comfortable castle, along with plenty of ladies-in-waiting, as well as knights and squires of honour, and with a few exceptions never show her face in public again.'

Castle Rising met the criterion and his mother did stay there, but not as a prisoner. 'The She-wolf of France' was able to enjoy all the privileges of a dowager queen when she lived at Castle Rising.

The tale is further embellished by accounts of her walking along a haunted tunnel. This linked the castle to the Red Mount Chapel at King's Lynn, her chosen place of worship. If the tunnel did exist, it would have been a round trip of some ten miles or more in a damp, smelly, confined space – surely not conducive to the temperament of a fiery, beautiful and imprisoned queen mother.

Contrary to popular belief, Queen Isabella did not die in Norfolk, but at Hereford Castle in 1358. However, her blood-curdling screams of solitude were claimed to have echoed through Castle Rising. There have been reports of hearing them in this century!

The foregoing and the queen's soubriquet most likely account for the legend of the hideous 'White Wolf of Castle Rising'. This was an apparition with the appearance of a 'giant wolf, white as driven snow, with two spectral eyes of fire and blood-dripping teeth'. Its ferocious howls could be heard on the battlements when the moon was full. Sometimes the beast was seen challenging a knight clad in 14th century armour to a fight. We shall never know the reason why, or whether the invitation was accepted, for all this happened a very long time ago.

CROMER

The Legend of the Church Rock

THE name 'Cromer' does not appear until the 13th century. Before then the village was known as 'Shipden'. By the end of the following century, most of the old village had finally toppled over the cliffs, the fate of many Norfolk coastal communities. All were at the mercy of the remorseless North Sea battering its way through their soft cliffs, until challenged by modern sea defences.

Some say the large submerged rock, known as Church Rock, which lies about a quarter of a mile from the shore, is not a rock at all. Apparently it can only be seen when conditions are right. The sea has to be clear and the tide exceptionally low. Then it appears to look like masonry. It has been suggested this is really the steeple of St Peter's church, which tumbled into the water all those years ago. Furthermore, past generations claimed to hear its bells ringing a warning when bad weather was approaching. Fishing boats took shelter and nets were hauled to safety. People knew only too well the danger that the angry waves brought, when the bells of Church Rock rang out.

The Lantern Men

THE Lantern Men, or Jack o' Lanterns, Will o' the Wisps, call them what you will, used to scare those who knew their reputation. They were thought to be little creatures who danced about, holding tiny lights to guide them through the dark. These nasty things caused harm and mischief to all who met them, leading travellers astray on dangerous and boggy ground.

In fact the little men and their lanterns were really flickers of self-igniting marsh gas, which flared up in the wetlands before the land was drained. Dry weather brought the Lantern Men out in droves! However, tell this to an old rustic and he would probably have spat to the east, to keep his luck intact.

Lady Cranworth was given the following account by an old Cromer fisherman. She was so impressed she had it printed in Volume 1 of the *Eastern Counties Magazine* in 1900.

'There's no saying what they will du to you, if that light on you! There was a young fellow coming home one evening and he see the Lantern Man coming for him and he run; and that run! and he run again; and that run again! Now there was a silly old man lived down there who didn't believe in none o' them things and this young fellow he run to his house and say, "O Giles, for Heaven's sake, let me in – the Lantern Man's coming!" And old Giles he say, "You silly fool, there ain't no such thing as a Lantern Man." But when he see the Lantern Man coming for him, Giles let the young fellow in, and that come for them two, till that was the beginer of a pint pot!

And old Giles, he thought he would play a trick on Lantern Man so he got a candle and held that out of the window on the end of a pole. And fust he held that out right high; and the Lantern Man, he come for that and he come underneath it. And then he held that out right low and the Lantern man he come up above it. And then he held that out right steady, and the Lantern Man he come for that and he burst it to pieces.

But they du say, if the Lantern Man light up you, the best thing is to throw yourself flat on your face and hold your breath.'

EAST DEREHAM

St Withburga

A MOST attractive sign spans the entry into the Butter Market from the High Street. It shows St Withburga confronting a huntsman and his dog, who are pursuing two deer.

Withburga was the youngest of the sainted daughters born to King Anna of the East Angles. Her sister, St Etheldreda, was the founder abbess of Ely, which grew into the glorious Ely Cathedral. Withburga founded the nunnery in East Dereham, situated in the heart of Norfolk.

The story behind the sign is that during a famine, two female deer came every day to a certain spot close to the religious house. They offered their milk to the hungry nuns, which was received with gratitude. When a huntsman gave chase to the animals, Withburga's prayers caused him to be killed when he fell from his horse. The two blessed creatures were safe to sustain the women until better times. This is said to be why the town is called 'Dereham'.

When Withburga died in around AD 654, she was interred in the nunnery graveyard. Her body did not decay and was later removed to the west of the graveyard in St Nicholas's parish church. The new shrine became a popular place of pilgrimage, where many miracles were witnessed.

All was well until King Edgar (AD 959–975) granted Dereham to the abbey at Ely. At that time its abbot, Brithnoth, was centralising the holy relics held within his jurisdiction. He wanted Withburga's remains. A licence was obtained from the king to remove them for safekeeping at Ely. However, he proceeded with caution. He was well aware that Dereham would not willingly relinquish such a valuable treasure, which attracted hordes of visitors who brought plenty of money with them. The loss would have a tremendous impact on the town.

In AD 974 Brithnoth and a few of his most trusted monks hatched a plan. They would visit Dereham to celebrate their possession of the place, but ostensibly ignore the holy relics. The abbot held his usual court of justice and laid on a great feast for the citizens, who ate and drank to excess. Ultimately they paid for their gluttony through the plunder of their precious relic.

When night fell the cunning visitors broke into Withburga's coffin. Satisfied that it contained her remains, which were still intact, they took their spoils to an awaiting carriage. The horses were pointed towards Brandon, some 20 miles away. Eventually the Dereham people, aware of the theft, gave chase. However, most of them were too drunk to even walk in a straight line and had no hope of saving their holy possession. The thieving monks had plenty of time in which to offload their bundle onto an awaiting boat and row away to Ely. They landed at Turburtsea Island, to the south of Queen Adelaide and received a joyful welcome. St Withburga was interred in the abbey church alongside her three holy sisters, Etheldreda, Sexburga and Ethelburga.

Dereham might have lost her remains, but her divine powers stayed behind. A healing well immediately bubbled up from her

29

old grave in the west of the churchyard. The miracles continued and the pilgrims still came to worship at this place.

Naturally the townspeople were infuriated by their abbot's conduct, but were powerless to act against their overlord. In time they became content with the now lucrative St Withburga's Well. You can still see it, along with the remains of a chapel which stood over this holy water. As for the holy relics taken to Ely, these were destroyed during the Reformation.

EAST RAYNHAM

The Brown Lady of Raynham Hall

SEVENTEENTH CENTURY Raynham Hall stands four miles south-west of Fakenham. It is said to be haunted by Lady Dorothy Townshend, known as 'The Brown Lady'. Lady Dorothy was a member of the wealthy Walpole family from Houghton, near King's Lynn. Her brother, Robert Walpole, 1st Earl of Orford, is generally regarded as the first English prime minister from 1721–1742 although the office was not recognised in his time. When her portrait was sold by Christies in the early 20th century, it was described as 'The Brown Lady, Dorothy Walpole, wife of the second and most famous Marquess Townshend'.

He was Charles 'Turnip' Townshend, a politician and agri-culturist who played an important role in introducing the turnip into England. It led the way to the 'Norfolk Four Course Rotation' which helped to revolutionise agriculture. Dorothy Walpole was only 15 years old when he, 22 years her senior, fell madly in love with her. She was said to have found him repugnant, so it was just as well that her family considered him unsuitable.

Townshend married another in 1699 and when she died in 1713, was finally accepted by Dorothy. A contemporary announcement states that Lady Dorothy died on 29th March

1726, aged 40 years. The cause was smallpox and she was mourned greatly by her husband. Shortly afterwards he resigned as Secretary of State and died in 1728 at the age of 64.

However, according to legend, this beautiful young woman was forced to marry him against her will. Their union was not happy. Townshend kept her locked up and treated her harshly. Finally, miserable and unloved, she fell down the grand staircase and was killed. 'Dolly' Townshend turned into the ghostly lady dressed in brown, the terror of Raynham Hall.

The Brown Lady appeared as an old woman dressed in a brown brocade dress, embroidered with gold. She wore a white lace cap and her complexion was the colour of ancient parchment. Her cheeks were hollow and her eyes sunken. Skinny, yellow-coloured arms poked out of her sleeves and her tiny feet were thrust into small-heeled shoes. The phantom was said to haunt the infamous grand oak staircase and was often seen outside the Belisarius Room.

Over the years there were many eye-witness accounts of her haunting. The following is what allegedly happened to three young male cousins of the family, who were visiting Raynham in the autumn of 1855.

By chance they bumped into the Brown Lady and chased her into a room. Trapping her there, they immediately locked the door from the inside and the key was removed. Suddenly the old woman vanished. They had a good look round, but she did not appear to be hiding. There was no earthly way in which she could have escaped. One of the threesome volunteered to guard the door all night, until the local constable could be summoned the next morning. Nobody could get in or out without his knowledge. Carpenters were ordered to remove the floorboards. The walls were tapped, the curtains examined, cupboards opened, nothing was left to chance. However, there was not a hint of the Brown Lady's presence.

All the time the three were adamant that they were not larking about. They had definitely imprisoned an old, yellow-skinned woman in the room. She was wearing a brown dress and a white lace cap. She had to be the Brown Lady!

ELLINGHAM

The Millers' Tale

IF you go past the 14th century church of St Mary, you will arrive at the beautifully restored Ellingham Mill. It sits in a valley on the borders with Suffolk, six miles north-west of Beccles.

At one time in the 19th century the mill was said to be operating twelve-hour shifts of two people, with the changeover at midnight. This strange tale began on a bright, moonlit night, when the men who told this supposedly true story were reporting for duty.

Their two mates were packing up to go home and their faces were whiter than the dust on their clothing. The men were reluctant to leave because they claimed to have seen a ghost standing on the other side of the mill bridge. The new couple were not amused. However, the two frightened mill-hands stayed put, insisting on showing their replacements the spot where the incident had taken place. They were certain that they had seen something 'which was as tall as a man, but misty and filmy looking'.

Eventually the four walked down to the water and the incident was recounted. The tree was pointed out by the bridge where the 'thing' had been hiding. Then it had drifted up the road and vanished out of sight. Satisfied from unburdening their ordeal, the two men went home. The new shift set about its work and the wheels turned. They did not believe the tale, but nevertheless agreed to keep a watchful eye on the spot, just in case. As expected, no 'filmy thing' came their way, reinforcing what they knew already. It was all poppycock!

The next night when they returned to work, there was no mention of ghosts. However, halfway through their shift, one of the men happened to look over the half-door and got a nasty shock. There, plain as a pikestaff, was the 'filmy thing' under the tree by the bridge. He raced upstairs for his mate, who grabbed a stout stick for protection. Together they stood by the door, looking down at the apparition. It stared back at them from the edge of the mill-stream, presumably with no intention of budging. The man with the stick was invited to knock it down.

Being a brave sort he threw open the door and raced over the bridge, holding his weapon like a Samurai warrior. In the heat of the moment he forgot that someone had placed a load of shingle down to give the horse traffic a better grip. His feet buckled under and he crashed heavily to the ground. The mysterious figure decided it was time to leave and drifted up the road in a swirl of mist and faded away.

The chap standing within the safety of the mill added the following statement to their account of that awful night:

'My partner came back very sore, and threw the stick in a corner. We didn't see the ghost again that night or ever afterwards. The governor's son or brother died out foreign about that time, and we always thought it was his ghost come back to have a look at the old place.'

No further suggestion of supernatural activity appears to be connected with Ellingham Mill. Was it really the spirit of the master's dead relation returning from 'out foreign' for one last look at the place? It is so beautiful, his need is quite understandable.

GREAT HOCKHAM

Matters of Witchcraft

DURING April 1857 a Norfolk magistrate wrote a letter to the *Times* newspaper concerning witchcraft. He quoted several instances, including the case of a 'well-to-do God-fearing yeoman farmer'. He referred to him as 'D' and said he lived at Hockham, seven miles north-east of Thetford.

The man was in bitter dispute with a neighbour concerning land, during which time his wife was suddenly struck with a strange illness. D blamed it on witchcraft. He was certain that he knew the culprit and applied to the magistrate to have her 'proved'. When asked how this should be done, he replied, 'Well sir, I thought you would have her swum.' This meant that if the accused was innocent she would sink and if guilty float. After more questioning from the bench, he gave the following reason for suspecting Mrs C of witchcraft:

> 'My wife was advised to send for a certain woman who is wonderful clever in these things. She came and told us to take some particular liquid and put it in a bottle with some of the hairs out of the noddle of my wife's neck and the parings of her finger nails and toe nails (these we cut quite close) and some old horseshoe nails. These you see, sir are little schemes which go from one generation to another, there's always something to be learned out of the weakest and ignorantest.
>
> Well, sir, we put the bottle on the fire and we waits while it's boiling and burning and when it bursts we look out of the window and the evil-disposed person stands before us. Last Friday night was a month that my wife did this and after she done it she got out of bed and she looked out of the window and there she saw Mrs C standing before the window at a most unsealable hour in the moonlight in an agony sort of state.'

The magistrate said he closed the interview by saying that he did not wish to hear any more nonsense. A few days later he was in an adjoining parish when a woman spoke to him about the case of Farmer D's wife.

> 'Only last Monday was a week,' she said, 'that there witch sent poor Mrs D up to the top of the house and then up the haystack and then on to the horses and made her even follow the plough on them. T'was all done first from jealousy. The people who could not have the land were determined that those who did get it should not enjoy it and so they set the old witch to disturb her.'

34

The magistrate remained unmoved by the story and one hopes that Mrs C was never 'proved'. He obviously dismissed the topic of witchcraft as outdated nonsense. Yet superstitious magic still had a role to play in the mid 19th century and beyond.

To illustrate this point, in 1923 a fruit farmer from my home village, near Wisbech, was pestered by what he thought was either a poltergeist or the Evil Eye. Whatever the source, things were flying around his house and falling off its walls. Mrs Holmes, the local wise woman or white witch, who lived at Birds Drove, was called in to cast out the influence. She brewed a commonplace spell, which was said to have worked. Like the bad Mrs C from Hockham, her recipe also included intimate personal objects. These were intended to make a vital link between the two subjects of the hex, the giver and the receiver. Therefore she took parings from the farmer's nails and those of his family, plus clippings from their hair and a number of apple pips, because of his living. She stirred them with up with his urine and poured the mixture into a bottle, which was sealed tight and put into the fire. All this was done in silence, another necessary ingredient. They say that when the bottle burst the Evil Eye, or whatever it was, went away.

Sadly the wise woman was found a few weeks later, drowned close to her home in a dyke containing six inches of water. People remember being told that the 'bad thing' had more than likely caused her untimely death. It had come back and sought revenge, but never troubled the farmer any more.

GREAT MELTON

The Spectral Bridesmaids

ACCORDING to tradition, this village, six miles east of Norwich, once witnessed a great tragedy when a party of bridesmaids were drowned. The accident was alleged to have occurred in either a bottomless pit or a pond. Had the former ever existed, it has miraculously been filled in. If, however, there is some grain of truth in the tale, there could be one pond which fits the description. This is on the Wymondham to Little Melton road at High Green, where a local resident claimed to have had a hair-raising experience not so long ago, even though it would appear that the original legend has faded from memory.

One night a long time ago, four young bridesmaids were seen returning from a wedding party. Nobody knew where they had been or where they were going. The girls were strangers, just passing through the village. Sadly, before they had left the parish they, their carriage, driver and horses fell into a pond. They sank to its bottom without trace.

One version of the story says that a highway robber was waiting for them behind some bushes. He reined in their horses, shot the coachman, then robbed the maidens. He concealed his crime by throwing them all into a bottomless pit which lay close by.

Another account puts the blame on the coachman. He was a drunkard who had got his lips around the wedding wine. He drove through Great Melton at a terrific speed, took the corner by the pond too quickly and all were drowned.

For many years thereafter a phantom coach and horses were said to speed down the road and around the bend where the accident occurred. Whoever dared catch a glimpse of its headless driver and the four headless bridesmaids could expect death, or at least bad luck to follow.

If the legend is based on a genuine accident, perhaps it occurred at the High Green Pond, which serves College Farm. Although not particularly deep, it is the largest in the village. Like the pond in the tale, it too is on a bend in the road, although not easily seen because it is screened by hedges. The owner thinks the highway may once have been routed closer to his water.

I am told that some 20 or 30 years ago, the now deceased Mr X who lived in the High Green area, had a nasty shock close to this spot. It has been pointed out by one who knew him that he was a practical, down-to-earth sort not given to imagining things. One evening X was walking by himself along the road, close to the bend where the College Farm pond lies. Suddenly, out of the blue, he said he heard horses galloping down the road. He told people it sounded like a team being driven at a ridiculous speed. He jumped onto the verge for safety, but claimed nothing passed him.

If Mr X had known the old story, he never shared it and did not link it with his personal experience. However, he swore on his honour that on that occasion he was the only person about. Perhaps he really was at the very place where the bridesmaids met their death many years ago.

GREAT YARMOUTH

The Egyptian Princess

ACCORDING to press reports, Great Yarmouth thrilled to rumours in 1913 that the mummified body of an Egyptian princess was haunting the graveyard of St Nicholas's church. The incident was claimed to have started when a nasty odour pervaded the Priory School, which stands close to the church. The school's assembly hall is the 13th century Priory Hall, which doubtless was once joined to St Nicholas's by cloisters.

The near-gagging smell suggested dead rats so floorboards were raised, but none were found. However, after many unpleasant days, the stink was finally traced to a casket containing the mummified remains of an Egyptian princess. The lid was opened and all was confirmed! The contents were quickly removed and buried in the churchyard, whilst the casket remained at the school.

A few weeks later the vicar and his family were reported to have been woken in the middle of the night. Someone was tapping on the vicarage door. He went to investigate, but whoever it was had gone away. This was repeated for several nights, then things returned to normal. However, workmen taking a short cut through the churchyard also heard knocking. This time it was coming from inside the church. They borrowed keys, thinking someone had been locked in. A thorough search showed the building to be empty and the men could find no reason for the noise.

A little later the annoying sounds returned to the vicarage and wild stories began to circulate. Eventually the police had to cordon off the church, which was alive with sightseers trying to catch a glimpse of 'the ghost of the Egyptian princess'.

Finally the smell returned to the classroom. A tiny fragment of the princess's leg was found lodged in the casket. This was interred alongside the other unusual remains and the knocking ceased. It was popularly assumed that the decaying mummy could not rest without her full complement of limbs. The ancient Egyptian princess is now intact and can sleep peacefully in the parish churchyard.

Old Scarfe

OLD SCARFE! Who is he? Some say he is the phantom dog from hell, better known as Black Shuck or Old Shuck. Others suggest he is the Hound of Odin, and his mythology came with the Viking invaders. There are still people who believe in him. Some cannot bear to speak his name, they have to call him the 'Hateful Thing'. However, he is better known as 'Old Scarfe' in this seaside town.

According to an old cutting filed in Great Yarmouth library, the spectre takes his name from the so-called wicked Baron Rudolph Scarfe. He was claimed to have lived in Germany in the 13th century. An evil man, who robbed and pillaged without remorse, his name became a by-word for everything bad and licentious. At last he was forced to flee and sought asylum in England. After a few years of travelling, he settled close to Burgh Castle, three miles west of Great Yarmouth.

Rotten to the core, Scarfe soon headed a violent gang of men who terrorised the neighbourhood. That was the time when tales of his past and present life were said to have made even the most hardened criminals shudder. Eventually he was killed by a brave knight. However, the baron was believed to be even too wicked for the Devil, who vowed to get rid of him. He changed him into a big black hell-hound, then swathed the beast in clanking chains and sent him back to earth. Satan commanded him to create eternal havoc!

For centuries Scarfe's name was used as a bugbear to frighten people. At midnight the superstitious were wary of crossing the bridge over the river Bure. This was the hour when the black dog rattled its chains as it walked to neighbouring Gorleston. It paid visits to Burgh Castle on a regular basis, frightening travellers who used the Yarmouth road. On occasions the beast was seen at the same hour, but in different places miles apart. Sometimes, with a Cyclops eye which glowed red, then changed to yellow. Others swore it had two eyes which changed colour. Some witnesses alleged its head was hovering over its body and there were reports of the dog being completely headless, but with one eye beaming in the dark.

There are many tales concerning this 'Hateful Thing'. In the 19th century a woman was returning from a Great Yarmouth inn. She said she got to within a few yards of her house in Blackfriars Road, when 'a horrible dog with starting eyeballs that gleamed like balls of fire' suddenly sprang out of the darkness. It placed its two huge forepaws on her shoulders, then stared her straight in the face, its foul breath striking her like the hot blasts of some great furnace. She screamed for help before falling senseless on the road.

By other accounts Old Scarfe occasionally turned up at the quay head on the west side of the river, this time without its chains, disguised as an abnormally large goat with big luminous horns. Although an awesome sight, it was less fearsome than when a dog. This apparition did not threaten humans, only farm stock.

To hear Black Shuck's, alias Old Scarfe's, howl is thought to presage death, if not on the spot then within the year. According to tradition, the hound walks each night over the bridge at Coltishall, eight miles north-east of Norwich. It has no head, but its eyes are the size of saucers and blaze in a most sinister fashion. Another of its infamous prowls is along the coast between Sheringham and Cromer. The thing also walks in various guises throughout East Anglia and the rest of Great Britain.

There are some people who still believe in the existence of Old Shuck. They have told me their tales. For example, take the experience of an elderly Fenland businessman. He is convinced the dog followed him during the Second World War when his motorbike had run out of petrol and he was compelled to walk in the dark from Southery to Downham Market, Norfolk. He even heard its chains, although, perhaps luckily, he did not turn round to look at the beast itself.

The other is a young woman who claims to have met it in the 1980s. She said the incident occurred when she and her young son were out alone at night. They were walking along the lonely Throckenholt Bank, at Parson Drove near Wisbech, just over the Norfolk border. The creature looked at them for a long time, staring with its one yellow eye, from behind a bush. When it finally raced off across the fields, she could see it was the size of a small calf. In her opinion there was no other explanation. It had to be Black Shuck!

GRESHAM

The Legend of the Grasshopper

THE wealthy Gresham family took their name from the village of Gresham, some five and a half miles south-west of Cromer. Sir Thomas founded the Royal Exchange in London, which was opened by Elizabeth I in 1568. The building is decorated with lots of grasshoppers and there is one on its magnificent weather-vane. This humble little insect came from Sir Thomas Gresham's crest and according to legend, this is how it got there.

A young girl, cradling her newborn babe, trudged along a country lane. When she was sure there was nobody about, she mounted a gate and abandoned the child in a field. Later on a boy who was out butterfly-hunting came up the lane, and heard a grasshopper from behind the hedge, chirping away as if fit to burst. He climbed over to see if he could catch it and found it beside the abandoned child, as if protecting it. The boy spared the insect and took the waif to a neighbouring farmhouse, where it was adopted by the farmer and his wife who were childless. They were good parents and said the grasshopper had deliberately alerted the young butterfly hunter, who had acted so responsibly.

The foundling grew into a good, clean-living man, but did not take over his guardian's farm. Instead he became a famous merchant. He was none other than Sir Thomas Gresham, the founder of the Royal Exchange! The great man was alleged to have adopted the grasshopper motif as a reminder of his humble beginnings. A romantic tale, but sadly untrue.

In item 98 of *Norfolk Notes and Queries* 1896, a correspondent gave his explanation for the grasshopper connection. He suggested that it was a play on the name 'Gresham'; 'gres' suggesting grass and 'ham' home. The 'grass-home' implies something which lives in the grass. Why not a grasshopper?

GRIMES GRAVES

Past, Present and Future?

GRIMES GRAVES are the largest and best known group of Neolithic flint mines in Britain. They lie some six miles north-west of Thetford off the A134 King's Lynn Road.

It is thought the Anglo-Saxons named the site. They were in this area about 1,500 years ago. The old mining holes were a great puzzle to them, they could not fathom their purpose, therefore they associated them with the supernatural and their chief god Woden. One of his identities was as 'Grim', 'Grimmer', or 'Grime', meaning 'the masked one'. The Saxons wore a grimer or cowled garment when working in the fields, to shield their faces from the sun. The word was also used to describe a mask. The suffix 'Graves' has no sinister implication, for a grave was their name for a man-made hole such as a mine, trench or ditch.

The Bronze Age burial mound at the rear of Grimes Graves

is known as 'Grimeshoe', pronounced 'Grimes Shoe'. This is a corruption of 'Grimes Hoe', which would have been 'Grimes Hill'. The Graves lie in the Hundred of Grimeshoe, where the Hundred Court is said to have met in medieval times.

Strange tales have arisen about this bleak and lonely area. However, those who are in a position to know claim that nothing out of the ordinary happens here. Except, perhaps, the following event which is said to occur from time to time.

Apparently a 'ripping yarn' concerning Grimes Graves was printed in the *Eagle*, a very popular boys' comic in the 1950s and 1960s. The tale involved a headless horseman, who created mayhem in the old mining tunnels. After lots of hair-raising adventures, each of which must have ended with the customary 'to be continued next week', the goodies triumphed over the baddies. This particular serial must have been tremendously popular, for I am told that on occasions mostly middle-aged *Eagle* fans arrive by coach at Grimes Graves. They come on a day's outing to re-enact the yarn, suitably togged out of course, and presumably minus the horse!

Who knows, their performance could turn into an accredited tradition, in the same way as many of our old customs have evolved.

HAPPISBURGH

The Happisburgh Smuggler

THE name of this village is pronounced 'Hazebra' and the legend of the smuggler is set in the 18th century. This was a time when smuggling played an important part in the economy of the Norfolk coastal area. Fighting and squabbling was rife amongst smugglers or 'free-traders', as illustrated in this gruesome tale.

One night waggons filled with contraband made their customary way from the beach, up through Cart Gap. They headed towards the village, about a mile to the north-west. A group of

42

men returning home late noticed the last one disappearing in the dark. It was followed by a stranger coming up the street from the direction of the Gap. Although moving at normal speed, they could see he had no legs and appeared to be headless. However, this was incorrect. His head was hanging by a skinny thread over his shoulders, complete with swinging pigtail. A pistol was thrust in the broad leather belt fastening his sailor's uniform. He clutched a parcel to his body and seemed to be unaware of the onlookers.

Their story was dismissed, so the men resolved to keep a close watch to see if the apparition returned. A few nights later they were rewarded.

The legless sailor once more floated along the street from the direction of Cart Gap. He still held his parcel close to him, but this time his head was correctly placed. The men followed him until he came to a well. The stranger stopped, threw his parcel down into the water and followed it in silence.

Once more the men were ridiculed when they told their tale. However, they remained resolute and eventually the well was searched. A volunteer went down, tied onto a piece of stout rope. When he had descended some 50 ft his lantern shone on a small piece of navy blue cloth. It was caught on a brick. He picked it up and his mates hauled him up, examined his find, then lowered him down. This time he carried a clothes prop so that he could probe the bottom of the well.

He returned with much to tell and on his third trip took a large hook tied to a piece of rope. He swung it round until it struck two objects which were long and firm. This was a pair of decomposing legs, with boots attached. The limbs had been hacked off at the thighs.

The young man refused a fourth expedition. Eventually a fisherman, encouraged with beer, was lowered with the same tackle. He came back clutching a heavy bundle of dripping cloth. It contained the body of a man whose head had been hacked off, except for a small thread of skin at the back of his neck. He was dressed in a sailor's uniform and a pistol was thrust into his wide leather belt.

A few weeks later, evidence of the murder of a sailor was unearthed near Cart Gap. The twin pistol of that belonging to the corpse in the well was found close to some gold coins.

Empty whisky bottles were strewn about and there were blood-stains on the sand. It was assumed this had been spilled during a quarrel between some smugglers. They had killed one of their own and cut him into pieces, to make it easier to hide him down the well. His killers were never discovered, neither was the identity of the Happisburgh Smuggler.

HICKLING BROAD

The Drummer Boy

HICKLING BROAD is famous for its pike fishing and the village gave its name to a special punt designed for wildfowling. It lies some ten miles north-west of Great Yarmouth, and has yet another claim to fame. According to legend a ghostly drummer boy used to skate over its frozen water.

It started at about the time of the battle of Waterloo in 1815, when a young soldier was home on leave. His girl friend lived across the water at Potter Heigham. However, her father disapproved of the boy's humble rank and forbade his daughter to see him. The lovers were forced to meet in secret and chose the lonely, marshy Swim Coots, on the Heigham side of the Broad.

The incident occurred one February. The weather had been harsh for a long time and Hickling Broad remained frozen. The boy had skated over to see his girl on many nights and all was well until the frost gave a little. He was warned to leave his skates at home and take the long way round, but time was precious to the lad. Off he went in the dark, without a thought of danger. When he reached the middle, the ice gave way and he plunged into the deadly cold water and was drowned. They say it was his ghost which skated on, to keep the lovers' rendezvous on the far bank.

For many years people claimed to see the drummer boy materialise at about 7 pm on icy February nights. They saw him skating over the ice, searching for the girl who still waited at Swim Coots. All the time he beat his drum and must have made a fearful sound. Indeed this was not his only music, for as reported by one who knew, 'He du whistle along tu, master'!

The Mad Black Canon

TUNNELS or subterranean passages are popular legends connected with religious houses. They invariably contained some sort of apparition or bogeyman, something nasty to scare the locals out of their wits on dark nights. The remains of the priory at Hickling are no exception and are associated with a ghostly cleric. From his description he appears to be on the verge of a nervous breakdown.

The priory was founded in 1185. It housed a prior and nine Augustinian canons, commonly called Austin Friars. The ruins stand to the north-east of the village, forming part of the Priory Farm buildings. The tunnel was reputed to commence at the site of the high altar and ran in a north-easterly direction for about half a mile or so. It finished in what is now a marsh drain, and was claimed to be haunted by an old, woefully thin monk. This was the Mad Black Canon!

Long ago he wandered around the priory precincts, carrying a pen and parchment scroll, as if trying to balance his accounts. Those who saw him said his figures did not appear to tally. He would scream with frustration, beat his breast and then start his sums over again. All the while this frustrated canon would be looking furtively around, as if he had something to hide. Finally he seemed to abandon the task and with his skinny face twisted with horror, would rush panic stricken into the underground passage. This was always at the priory end. He exited where the marsh drain now is and vanished into the dark.

One night some brave sceptics set out to explore the tunnel, in an attempt to debunk the Mad Black Canon tale. Unfortunately they only added to the nightmare. They said he had met them halfway through, his face twisted with rage. Presumably the living and the dead exited from different ends of the tunnel!

It has been suggested that, when alive, this canon falsified the priory accounts. His spirit was a dire reminder to all clerks who sought a peaceful after-life. Do not fiddle the books in this one!

HOLT

The Holt Owls

NORFOLK is rich in place nicknames and the people from Holt were once known as 'The Holt Knowers' (or 'Know-alls'). The inference is that its citizens were a bit daft, for the names are old! Happily this pretty market town, which lies some nine miles south-west of Cromer, remains unmoved. It is obviously proud of its owl stories, for the birds have a high profile about the place. One is even carved on the town sign.

Some local men, it is said, were bringing back the cattle from their summer grazing on the Salthouse Marshes. They saw an owl lying concussed at the side of the road. The injured creature was picked up and taken to the market place and placed in an open-topped animal pen for safekeeping. The men of Holt were greatly puzzled when the bird flew away. How had it happened? Why were bars put on pens, if not to prevent their occupants from escaping!

Another yarn tells us that the wise men of Holt, having caught an owl, placed it in the waterspout of the church tower. They thought it would be drowned in the next rain. Imagine their surprise when they saw it fly out at the top!

In his book *Ghosts and Witches* published by Batsford in 1954, J Wentworth Day gives another 'Holt Knowers' anecdote told to his friend who lived in a house called 'Three Owls'. An old man who had probably never left the locality, was convinced that Noah's Ark had come to rest on Mulbarton Common (south west of Norwich) because 'Aren't this the highest bit o' ground for miles round?' He went on to say that when the Devil saw the Ark, he got into his punt and came alongside just as Noah was opening the window to let the dove out. 'Nice mornin' arter the rain,' says Old Nick, but Noah noticed his tail curled under the water and he shouted out, 'You go to hell,' and banged the window down!

HORNING

The Ghost of the Ferry Inn

COME summertime, Horning is one of the busiest boating centres on the Norfolk Broads. Its attractive cottages and boating lodges with thatched boathouses please both road and water traffic. About a mile downstream from the village centre you will find the equally popular Ferry Inn. This fronts onto the river Bure, which makes it an ideal stopping-off point for thirsty boat crews. Until fairly recent times a ferry boat used to take people across the river from that point.

According to a notice displayed in the bar, the place is haunted by a young woman. However, neither the manager nor his staff have seen her. She is said to be aged about 25 years and wears a green cloak. The notice says she glides through the bar and then vanishes into the river. On other occasions she is seen walking mournfully along the river Bure, close to the solitary abbey ruins at Ludham. Her face is deathly white, yet still beautiful.

During the 15th century, a mead storehouse serving the abbey stood on the site of the Ferry Inn. Presumably an inn was eventually built around the old store, which evolved into the present large building. The woman in green is said to have been murdered by some drunken monks who dumped her body into the river to conceal their crime. Was a woman murdered here by roistering monks, who had more than their fair share of mead? Or was it all a tale, perhaps, to lend atmosphere to the Ferry Inn, both ancient and modern!

HORSEY MERE

Hag Stones and Witches

HORSEY MERE is off the B1159 Cromer to Caister road and adjoins the restored water pump, which is a splendid landmark. There is an old saying, 'Horsey pike, none like'. In the days of public fishing the mere was famous for its well-stocked waters and its pike – if you ever dared to go there. This solitary place was said to be the haunt of witches. They used the lonely bank between it and the sea for their unholy sabbaths.

It is still home to adders and to the plant belladonna, which according to Gerard, the Elizabethan herbalist, 'causeth sleep, troubleth the mind, bringeth madnesse if a few of the berries be inwardly taken, but if moe be given they also kill and bring present death'.

This plant was one of the ingredients of witches' flying ointment, an hallucinatory potion which gave the user the impression of flight. Some said the mixture was made by the Devil himself. He made the witches a gift of it in return for a kiss on his posterior. However, by whatever method, fly they did around Horsey Mere, or so it was reported, even in the 19th century. As bold as brass, they went their way over this then God-forsaken place, its only sounds the booming sea behind the bank and the cry of birds.

Local people said they saw them up in the night sky, astride their broomsticks or the cleft branch of a tree. They heard them shrieking and yelling in a terrifying fashion as they headed towards their sabbath. This act was a reversal of what was practised in a church. The devout met mostly by day to offer worship on their knees to an invisible God in a consecrated building, witches and warlocks met together at night to pay homage to a visible Devil in a lewd manner. And they flew over Horsey Mere on their outward and homeward journeys. At times they pitched down to do mischief.

It was said that witchcraft was rampant in those days. There were many good people who had seen old hags turning themselves into pretty girls, to entice young men to their folly. It was generally agreed that most would rather cut off their hands than venture near that place of evil worship by night.

At the end of the 19th century a brave man from neighbouring Sea Palling tried to hire a boat on the lake for some night fishing. Nobody would oblige until after the full moon. They believed that if the witches flew overhead, the boat would be cursed and its occupants drowned.

No wonder evil had such a high profile, given the lonely environment and poor accessibility, even to the next house, let alone hamlet. It was probably easy to accept as truth the notion that wicked people mixed up spells from boiled children, murdered before their baptism.

Equally one cannot doubt the great security offered by good-luck talismen. These included safe-keeps, such as verses copied from the Bible or words written by the local wise man or woman. The paper was often crumpled up and placed in a nutshell, for extra safety in the pocket. Hag stones were considered to be an effective protection from evil and did not depend upon literacy skills. These ordinary stones with a natural hole through them represented the 'All Seeing Eye', which deterred wickedness. They were often hung over people's beds and in the stables, to keep the night hag or 'night-mare' from causing mischief.

Hag stones are quite plentiful on the beach at Horsey, not far from where the witches were said to land. Doubtless these crow-black hags keep well away from the hollow 'eyes' which still gaze unblinkingly from that great stretch of sand.

HOUGHTON HALL

The Ghost of Houghton Hall

HOUGHTON HALL is the grandest of all the Norfolk country homes. It was built in the 1730s by Sir Robert Walpole, generally regarded as the first prime minister of England. 'Bob of Lynn', so called because he was MP for King's Lynn, was delighted with the house, but not the view. He did not wish to look onto Houghton village, which was almost wholly contained within his park. Therefore, he built a new village out of sight and pulled the old one down. It is to be found 13 miles east of King's Lynn, off the A148.

Unsurprisingly, a spectre is linked with the hall. One would have hoped that the grandest residence in Norfolk would have had a ghost of equal status. Something above the usual run of the supernatural, or at least one which it could have called its own! However, Houghton's spectre appears to have flitted between it and Raynham Hall. This was the ghost of Sir Robert's sister, Dorothy Walpole, known better as the Brown Lady, who had married 'Turnip' Townshend of Raynham.

She was even said to have been seen at Houghton by George IV, then Prince Regent, when he was a guest of the Marquess of Cholmondeley. The royal visitor was occupying the Velvet State Bedchamber, her favourite haunt. His Royal Highness was not pleased. He declared to his host whilst demanding a new room, 'I will not pass another hour in this accursed house, for I have seen what I hope to God I may never see again!' The prince had seen an apparition which looked like 'a little lady all dressed in brown with dishevelled hair and a face of ashy paleness'. A perfect description of the Brown Lady.

The Norfolk Riddle

A LARGE number of political broadsheets were published in the early 18th century. The object of their usually anonymous authors was to make swipes at the leading politician of the day. The following, which is entitled *The Norfolk Riddle, explain it if you can*, is thought to be a satire on Sir Robert Walpole.

It makes more sense if you have a brief potted history of Robert Walpole's background. In the 12th century his wealthy family moved from Walpole in Marshland, near Wisbech, to Houghton, near King's Lynn. In 1701 he was returned to Parliament for the pocket borough of Castle Rising and the next year was elected MP for King's Lynn, continuing to represent the borough. 'Bob of Lynn' was a Whig. In 1712 the Tories made a charge of corruption against him which resulted in his imprisonment in the Tower of London for several months. However, this did not stop him from going back into the government as First Lord of the Treasury and then Chancellor of the Exchequer. Walpole went on to become the first Prime Minister of England.

Speculation regarding his source of wealth grew when he built his new mansion at Houghton. It was the finest in the county and filled with priceless treasures, the cost of which could not have come from his family fortune alone.

The Norfolk Riddle was published in the 1730s and printed so the words formed a square, radiating from the middle.

'In Norfolk once, there was a Thing that look'd as great as any King, and yet he was no King indeed, tho' by him all things were Decreed; He made each one to him Submit, Abroad, at home, as he thought fit; Yet this immense prepost'rous Beast, Destroy'd whole Thousands at the least; He never thought he had enough, His greedy Maw he so did Stuff; Untill he ready was to burst, Yet after more he still did Thirst, and headlong on, he still did run In the same Course that he begun: If Norfolk do's such Monsters breed How shall we do them for to Feed? Worse than a Dragon he destroys, the Country daily he annoys, Some, like himself, him Homage pay, And are Delighted in his ways, But time will come to feel the Sting, as well as cut off this vile Thing, who does upon us so much Prey, With Sport and Pastime e'ery Day; Defying those, that would perswade The rest who basely he betray'd, to pull this Monster from the Head, Who has so many Mischief's bred: This Devil like, more than a Man! Explain this RIDDLE if you can.'

Despite his political success, Sir Robert Walpole, 1st Lord Orford, remained a countryman at heart. His big square figure and vulgar good-humour were said to make him appear more like a common country squire than the head of government. His real love was for the table, the bottle and the chase. He rode as hard as he drank and never completely lost his Norfolk accent. Even in moments of political peril, the first despatch he would open would be the letter from his gamekeeper.

HUNSTANTON

The Shipwrecked King

THE remains of a chapel stand on top of the cliffs by the lighthouse at St Edmund's Point. The building was erected in 1272 by the monks of Bury St Edmunds, Suffolk. It commemorates the landing of the German boy Edmund, who arrived at this spot from Germany in AD 854. He came to England to inherit the throne of East Anglia.

According to legend, Edmund was shipwrecked off the coast. However, he managed to reach the shore, where he knelt in prayer and thanked God for his safe deliverance. Immediately a spring of clear water gushed from the spot. The future king stayed here for a year and founded a settlement which became known as Hunstanton, from 'honey', as signifying power and sweetness. It still enjoys its nickname 'Sunny Hunny'!

In AD 855 Edmund was crowned king, at the age of 15. The ceremony was performed by Bishop Humbert of Elmham, Norfolk. The new monarch was a devout Christian and popular ruler, whose kingdom comprised Norfolk and Suffolk. However, his reign was fraught with Danish invasions, and he was murdered near Thetford, at Hoxne, Suffolk in AD 870.

He became a Christian martyr and the first patron saint of England. Many of the painted screens in East Anglian churches contain his likeness. St Aethelbert's at Hoxne has some old bench ends, one of which depicts St Edmund's head being carried off by a wolf. Likewise, at Walpole St Peter's, near Wisbech, there is another fine bench end showing St Edmund's head guarded by a wolf (see Reedham).

INGHAM

The Ghostly Battle

INGHAM lies on the northern edge of Broadland, on the B1151 Stalham to Sea Palling road. It used to have the nickname 'Sleepy Ingham' because life there was so dull! Each day was indistinguishable from another. To illustrate the point, they say that one day a man dressed himself in his Sunday clothes on Monday and went to church!

However, according to tradition, something unusual did occur in this village on one night of each year. This was when the ghosts of Sir Roger de Bois and Sir Oliver de Ingham did battle with a foreign warrior.

At the east end of the nave of Holy Trinity church, is the table tomb with effigies of Sir Roger and his wife Margaret, dated 1300. On the northern side of the sanctuary Sir Oliver's effigy is recumbent on a bed of pebbles. This is dated 1343. It is said that on the night of 2nd August each year, the images of the two knights changed to flesh and blood.

Together, they walked slowly and deliberately out of the church and headed for Stalham Broad. Here they fought with a soldier with an Eastern appearance and the combat was long and savage. When the two knights had slain their opponent, they returned and resumed their stony positions in Holy Trinity church.

Perhaps they were re-enacting a deadly battle from the Crusades? The reason has been forgotten, even if it were ever known. The two brave knights do not appear to have stretched their legs within memory. Instead they sleep as God intended, within the shadow of the tall church tower.

IRSTEAD

Jack o' Lantern

TOWARDS the end of the 19th century, Mrs Lubbock, the local wise woman or 'white witch', told a strange story. She said that before the Irstead enclosure in 1810, Jack o' Lantern was seen roaming about the place. This was always on 'roky' (misty) nights and often at a place called Heard's Holde. This is in Alder Carr Fen Broad on the Neatishead side, shown as Alderfen Broad on OS map 134 TG354194. A man called Heard, a hardened criminal, had been drowned there.

The old lady had often seen the creature at this place, 'rising up and falling and twistering about, and then up again'. She thought this was Heard's spirit, still capable of doing harm. 'If anyone were walking along the road with a lantern at the time when he appeared, and did not put out the light immediately, Jack would come against it and dash it to pieces.' She said that a gentleman who made mock of him and called him 'Will of the Wisp' was riding on horseback one evening in the adjoining parish of Horning, 'when he came at him and knocked him off his horse'.

When Mrs Lubbock was young, her father often told the tale of when he was returning home from a spending spree at the end of harvest. He was accompanied by an old man who whistled and jeered at Jack. The sprite followed them all the way home. When they entered the brave man's house it 'torched up at the windows'.

The Neatishead people were greatly annoyed with its tricks and determined to lay it. They knew its route, as it always went to places frequented by Heard when he was alive. Three men attempted the deed by reading verses from the Bible. The apparition always kept one verse ahead of them, to thwart their efforts. That is until a boy brought a pigeon which he placed alongside Jack o' Lantern. It looked down at the bird and lost its verse. Then she said they bound its spirit and it was no more trouble.

As mentioned in the Cromer tale, Jack o' Lanterns, alias

Will o' the Wisps, were really flickers of self-igniting marsh gas, which flared up especially in hot weather. They disappeared when the wetlands were drained. Many regarded them as evil influences. A common belief was their power to lure travellers to their death on dark nights. Drawn to the sparkles like moths to a lantern, travellers left the safe path to seek their source. This took them out into the deadly bogs and swamps, from which they sometimes never returned.

ISLINGTON

The Bailiff's Daughter of Islington

AT first sight Islington, known also as Tilney cum Islington, appears to be a tiny hamlet. However, as often happens in Fenland, the parish covers a very wide area.

Islington in Norfolk and Islington in Middlesex are both said to be the setting of the ballad concerning 'The Bailiff's Daughter'. This romance tells us about a rich boy who falls in love with a poor girl. Their misunderstanding leads to a long separation, which ends with marriage vows.

Bishop Percy states in his *Reliques of Ancient English Poetry* Vol III that the setting of this popular old ballad is probably Islington in Norfolk. Yet there is the person said to have represented 'a squier minstrel of Middlesex', who made a speech before Elizabeth I at Kenilworth in 1575, in which he declared 'how the worshipful village of Islington (was) well knooen too bee one of the most auncient and best tounz in England, next to London'. This was in defence of the other Islington being the subject of the song. There is no proof either way, so like the good bishop and many others, I shall settle for the isolated parish close to King's Lynn.

The ballad tells us that a squire's young son fell in love with the bailiff's shy daughter. She did not believe his declarations and in turn showed him no feeling. When his family and friends

55

discovered his passion for this lowly girl, they packed him off to London to take up an apprenticeship. However, after seven years away from home, he was still shedding tears for the girl whom he believed had thought so little of him.

> 'Then all the maids of Islington
> Went forth to sport and playe,
> All but the bayliffes daughter deare;
> She secretly stole awaye.
>
> She pulled off her gowne of greene,
> And put on ragged attire,
> And faire London she would go
> Her true love to enquire.'

The weather was hot, the distance long. Overcome with tiredness, she rested on a grassy bank. By chance the squire's son rode by, he being unaware of her identity and she of his. The girl begged a penny from him and he replied:

> 'Before I give you one penny, sweet-heart,
> Praye tell me where you were borne.
> At Islington, kind sir, say'd shee,
> Where I have had many a scorne.'

He asked if she had news of the bailiff's daughter and was told she had died a long time ago. The young man was distraught:

> 'If she be dead, then take my horse,
> My saddle and bridle also;
> For I will into some farr countrye,
> Where noe man shall me knowe.'

At long last the bailiff's daughter knew that the squire's son loved her. She cried:

> 'O staye, O staye, thou goodlye youthe,
> She standeth by thy side;
> She is alive, she is not dead,
> And readye to be thy bride.'

Then the joyful youth exclaimed:

> 'O farewell griefe, and welcome joye,
> Ten thousand times therefore;
> For nowe I have founde mine owne true love,
> Whom I thought I should never see more.'

If the ballad is based on truth, I wonder if the heroine's father was employed by the owner of the now altered 13th century Islington Hall? This is three miles from the parish sign and stands next to the ruined St Mary's church. Its approach is by trackway off the A47 King's Lynn road, opposite the road to Tilney All Saints church. The hall looks out over the fields to the south and onto the heronry in Three Acre Field. All around is arable land, which accounts for most of Islington. Apart from the re-routing of the river, the place has changed little since the bailiff's daughter went to London.

KING'S LYNN

Margery Kempe

MARGERY KEMPE was born in the town in around 1372. After experiencing a conversion following a period of insanity, she was described as 'Lynn's most famous spiritual genius'. In 1441 the Archbishop of Canterbury granted this mystic an interview. Her marriage to a local merchant, John Kempe, had taken place 21 years earlier but mothering 14 children did not prevent Margery from travelling all over the Continent, visiting Rome and the Holy Land. Although illiterate, between about 1432 and 1436 she dictated her memoirs. This became *The Book of Margery Kempe*, which is written in the third person singular and was the first biography to be written in English.

Much of Mistress Kempe's time was spent wailing, gnashing her teeth and generally annoying people. On her trip to Jerusalem she made such a racket that her fellow pilgrims left her behind. However, attitudes towards this strange woman changed in Norfolk when Lynn was engulfed in a great fire. This was thought to have occurred on 23rd January 1420/1421. The Guildhall was destroyed and the flames were threatening nearby St Margaret's church, described as 'a stately place and richly honoured', when it was saved by Margery Kempe's intercession.

As she says in her book, '. . . notwithstanding that at other times they could not endure her crying and weeping because of the plentiful grace that our Lord worked in her, on this day, in order to lessen their physical danger, they allowed her to cry and weep as much as she liked . . .' Indeed they begged her to continue, hoping that through her tears the Lord would be merciful to the town.

Roger Spryngolde, thought to be the parish priest, asked if he should take the Holy Sacrament to the flames or not. She told him to do so, 'For our Lord Jesus Christ told me it will be well.' When he replaced it in the church, the sparks were already flying around its exterior. Margery rushed outside and cried with a loud voice and further weeping, 'Good Lord, make everything all right, and send down some rain or storm that may through your mercy quench this fire and ease my heart.'

Then she went inside and saw how the sparks were coming into the choir through the lantern of the church. She cried again for grace and mercy. Soon after, three men came to her with snow on their clothes. They said, 'Look, Margery, God has shown us great grace and sent us a fair snowstorm to quench the fire with. Be now of good cheer, and thank God for it.'

It was generally agreed that through her pleading, Margery Kempe was responsible for the change in the weather and saved Lynn from even greater destruction by fire. She is said to have died in 1440, when she was about 68 years old.

The Red Mount Chapel Fiddler

THIS tiny little chapel was built in 1485 and its roof is often compared to that of King's College Chapel in Cambridge. It is also known as the Chapel of Our Lady's Hill and stands on a mound in St James Park.

According to tradition, pilgrims to Walsingham used it as a resting place as they passed through Lynn. Queen Isabella, 'The She-wolf of France' (see Castle Rising) was also said to have visited it for worship via a so-called secret tunnel. This was claimed to link the chapel with the castle at Castle Rising, but there is no proof of its existence.

Another legend surrounds the mound. It is said that at an unknown time, a drunken fiddler named Curtis decided to explore its tunnel. Traditionally secret tunnels were usually connected with fear and evil. Why Curtis should have wished to enter its depths is anyone's guess, but the story says he did. His pet dog went with him and they were never seen again. Both were assumed to be trapped and left to their fate.

Later his escapade was the subject of a terrible ballad composed in the late 19th century. It is called *The Fiddler and the Imps* and commences:

> 'At the town of Lynn,
> Did the cave begin,
> And to Castle Rising went.
>
> A bottle of grog
> He took, and his dog,
> And fiddled right merrilie.'

There are 48 more verses, which are enough to drive anyone underground!

However, the hero is not forgotten. On occasions he is still heard playing his tunes, with the dog whimpering to get out.

LAKESEND

A Lousy Trick!

THEY said that Mrs Reeves was a witch. She lived at Lakesend, a hamlet some nine miles south-west of Downham Market. The following is taken from the Folklore Society's publication *Folklore*

Vol V V.50 1939. Mr Crawford lived close to Mrs Reeves and this is what he had to say about an incident which happened in 1881:

'Her daughter had done wrong an' I spuk the truth about it an' because I spuk the truth she said she'd do I don't know what to me an' my mate. I come hum lousy one night an' went to work next day. I was yardman at the time, it was the first year we were married – 58 year ago – an there was another young man workin' wi' me.

'He come up at dinner-time, I say to him, "Don't you come near me, Twister, 'cause I'm lousy." An' I say to this young man, "If I don't get rid o' these lice before I git hum I'll shake hell over her."

'When the young man went hum this old woman was in his mother's house. He say to his mother, "Mother, old Bob Crawford is lousy" . . . and he told his mother just what I said at dinner-time. She (Mrs Reeves) heard it and went hum and was took bad, an' when I went hum my head was as clean as it is now.'

Mrs Crawford added that although she could feel lumps under her husband's skin during the bewitchment, she could see nothing.

The Man who Sold his Wife

THE incident which started the ball rolling was said to have happened round about the winter of 1876. It was after a man sold some pigs to a butcher, who was then late in settling his account. The dealer banged on his door and demanded immediate payment. The debtor assured him that it had been sent in the post a long while ago. Private investigation proved that the postman had stolen the money, so he was reported to the police and given the sack.

That winter was harsh and the ice held out for 16 glorious weeks. Like most Fenmen, the light-fingered postman was a competent skater and made good use of the weather. He was out most days on his 'Fen Runners', which were skates with an upturned curved blade. They made you think of a sultan's footwear. Races were held on the nearby flooded Welney Washes. Prizes of beef, beer, pigs, gloves and guaranteed feminine approval were there for the winning. It was during an especially exhilarating contest that the police came down and arrested the thief. He finally confessed to his crime and served a five year stretch in gaol.

When he had done his time, he returned to Lakesend. By then his lonely and attractive wife had taken up with another man. Although still living in the marital home, she said she intended moving in with her lover when the time was right. The cuckolded husband adjudged it to be then and there. He would have nothing more to do with her. But she was not going to get off that lightly. He made a halter which he put around her neck and led her four miles up the road to New Bridge at Upwell. She was offered up for auction. There were plenty of onlookers, but only one bidder. This was her lover, who brought her for a quart of beer!

Selling wives by auction was not an uncommon practice. In his book, *The Mayor of Casterbridge*, Thomas Hardy has Susan Henchard and her little daughter auctioned off to a sailor for five guineas. As her drunken husband says, 'I take the money, the sailor takes you!' Susan agrees to the transaction, although the new man is a stranger to her. He could not be worse than her bad-tempered spouse.

Presumably the Lakesend lover and his mistress thought they too had a good bargain, as did the avenged husband.

LANGLEY

The Prophetic Cross

THERE was an old prophecy, of unknown origin, surrounding the stone market cross which once stood in a meadow close to Langley Abbey. This marked the site of a weekly market.

The abbey was founded in 1198 for Premonstratensian canons, known as White Canons from their white robes. Its remains can still be seen on the edge of the marshes, close to the river Yare, twelve miles south-east of Norwich.

According to legend this cross had been subjected to abuse and vandalism for many years. It was decided to remove it for safekeeping to Langley Park, the grounds of Langley Hall, which is east of the village. This was originally the home of the Beauchamp Proctor family and is now a private school. However, tradition warned that should the cross be moved, a great conflagration would engulf its new surroundings.

The prediction was unheeded and the cross uprooted. No sooner was the task complete than the old prophecy was said to come true. That night the cry of 'Fire!' was raised. Ominous clouds of thick black smoke were seen gushing out of the mid 18th century mansion. The villagers rushed to quench the flames and managed to save the hall, and Lady Beauchamp, from destruction.

Some of the park has since been cultivated and the cross now stands in arable land. This is south-west of the hall, next to Thicks Plantation and marks the place where the boundaries of four villages meet. The ancient prophecy has been fulfilled. All remains quiet at Langley Hall.

LITTLE WALSINGHAM

The Dream of Lady Richeldis

THE first shrine of Our Lady of Walsingham was founded over 900 years ago, since when it has remained a popular place of pilgrimage. At one time this village six miles north of Fakenham attracted more devout visitors than Canterbury.

It is said to have started with a dream. The dreamer was the Lady Richeldis de Faverche, widow of the lord of the manor of Walsingham. One night in 1061 the Virgin Mary visited her in her sleep. Lady Richeldis was instructed to have a replica of the Holy House of Nazareth built in her then tiny hamlet. This was the house in which Mary had been told by the Archangel Gabriel that she was to bear the Son of God. The original Nazarene dwelling was claimed to have been miraculously transported by angels to the Sancta Casa at Loretto.

The Blessed Mary explained that a fresh spring of water would mark the spot where the house was to be built. The water appeared and a simple shrine was built over it. However, for no apparent reason, the building was continuously disturbed. Lady Richeldis was anxious and spent one entire night in prayer. The next morning the tiny building had been moved, as if by God's hand, to the site of twin wells some 200 ft west of the original site.

Then another miracle occurred. This time the statue of Our Lady of Walsingham suddenly appeared in the shrine. She granted many miracles and most kings of England from Henry III to Henry VIII visited the shrine. Pilgrims who chose to walk the last mile barefoot, placed their shoes in the 14th century Slipper Chapel in the neighbouring parish of Houghton St Giles. Henry VIII, who was yet to order the destruction of the monasteries, humbled himself in this fashion.

Pilgrims came in such great numbers that the road to the Holy House became one of the main highways in England. The cluster of stars in the night sky known as the Milky Way, was sometimes called the 'Walsingham Way'. It was thought to point to England's Nazareth, whose myriad roads resembled this galaxy.

The statue of Our Lady remained at the shrine until the time of the Dissolution in the 1530s, when it was taken to London and burned at Chelsea.

The Elizabethan ballad *A Lament for Walsingham*, describes the bitter deed so beautifully. It ends:

> 'Oules do scrike where the sweetest himnes
> Lately were songe,
> Toades and serpents hold their dennes
> Where the palmers did throng.

Weepe, weepe O Walsingham,
Whose days are nightes,
Blessings turned to blasphemies,
Holy deeds to dispites.

Sinne is where our Ladie sate,
Heaven turned is to hell,
Sathan sittes where our Lord did swaye,
Walsingham oh farewell.'

LUDHAM

The Abbot for Life

THE ruins of St Benet's-at-Holme Abbey lie alongside the river
Bure. You can reach them either by boat or the narrow concrete
road which leads over the marshes. This is between Ludham
and Johnson Street.

King Canute is said to have built the abbey in about 1016
and granted the order his manors of Horning, Neatishead
and Ludham. Other owners were equally generous. St Benet's
became one of the wealthiest abbeys in England. By the end of
the 13th century it owned property in 76 Norfolk parishes.

Nowadays the old ruins are perhaps best known for the story
of the man who was made 'Abbot for Life'. The incident is
said to have happened at the time of the Norman invasion.
Being in such an isolated position and so close to the river,
the building was constructed more like a castle than an abbey.
The monks had held out against the Norman army for over
four months. They could have continued their resistance for a
lot longer, but for a 'rotten apple' in their midst. This was the
lowly, unordained caretaker, who had delusions of grandeur.
According to the story, his ambitions turned him into one of
the undead.

The Normans were about to give up their attack. However,

in a last-ditch attempt to gain control, they tried a trick. A messenger with a white flag was sent to deliver a letter to the abbot urging his surrender. Before his audience with the great man, another note was given to the caretaker. It said that the Norman leader wished to speak with him, and he guaranteed his safety. The foolish servant was flattered and later followed the messenger back to his leader. A tempting offer was made. If he would help them to capture the abbey, he would be made its abbot for life. There was nothing to lose. If the monks refused their allegiance to the new abbot, they would be killed by the Normans. On the other hand, if they refused to surrender to the enemy, they would still be killed, including the caretaker!

The bargain was struck. That night the traitor ensured that the massive bolt securing the main door was pulled back. The soldiers rushed in and the holy brethren put up little resistance. A truce was soon agreed and the abbot deposed. The following morning the caretaker was paraded before the community. As promised, he was created the abbot of St Benet's-at-Holme for life. The monks were furious, yet powerless to resist. However, there was no need, for their new principal, still dressed in his robes of high office, was dragged off by his Norman 'friends' and hanged. According to tradition, this happened either from the lowest window of the bell tower, or possibly from the west gate. The latter was later incorporated into the now derelict 18th century mill. The Normans had no use for a confirmed traitor, so the original abbot was reinstated and life returned more or less to normal.

At the time of the Dissolution some five centuries later a deal was struck with the predatory Henry VIII. All St Benet's assets were made over to the Crown and the last of its 37 abbots was appointed Bishop of Norfolk. The two offices were combined and remain so. By an Act of Parliament the abbot was charged to maintain at least twelve monks to continue the tradition of worship and service. This was the only religious house in England to escape dissolution. Each year the Bishop of Norwich holds a service here on the first Sunday in August.

However, it is said that if you visit these ruins late at night, be warned. Given the solitude and the noise of the night creatures you too may hear the awful screams which come from the ghostly Abbot for Life, dangling from his makeshift gibbet.

MANNINGTON HALL

Dr Jessop Meets a Ghost

ON 10th October 1879, the well known antiquarian, Dr Augustus Jessop, set out to visit Lord Orford at 15th century Mannington Hall. This is situated about two miles from Corpusty. He was going to work on some rare books contained in the library. He was also going to see a ghost, but of course did not know it at the time. Even if he had, it probably would not have bothered him. Dr Jessop appears to have remained very much in charge of the experience, which was reported in the *Athenaeum* of January 1880.

Everyone was in bed by 11 pm and the servants had been dismissed. The scholar took advantage of the quiet and settled to work in the luxuriously appointed ante room off the library. There was a good fire in the huge fire-place, with its great old fashioned chimney. Jessop was pleased. He said he was a chilly creature and sat himself at a table with the fire-place to his left. A small pile of books was placed at his right hand and he worked without interruption until 1.30 am. Suddenly he was aware of a large white hand some twelve inches from his elbow.

The article continues:

'Turning my head, there sat a figure of a somewhat large man, with his back to the fire, bending slightly over the table and apparently examining the pile of books that I had been engaged upon. The man's face was turned away from me, but I saw his closely-cut reddish-brown hair, his ear and shaven cheek, the eyebrow, the corner of his right eye, the side of the forehead and the large high cheek bone. He was dressed in what I can only describe as a kind of ecclesiastical habit of thick corded silk or some such material, close up to the throat, and a narrow rim or edging of satin or velvet, serving as a stand-up collar, and fitting close to the chin.'

The hand which had first caught the eye of the doctor was claimed to have looked remarkably like the hand of Velasquez's 'Dead Knight' in the National Gallery.

'I looked at my visitor for some seconds and was perfectly sure that he was not a reality. A thousand thoughts came crowding upon me, but not the least feeling of alarm or even uneasiness; curiosity and a strong interest were uppermost. For an instant I felt eager to make a sketch of my friend, and I looked at a tray on my right for a pencil; then I thought, "Upstairs I have a sketch book; shall I fetch it?"

There he sat, and I was fascinated – afraid, not of his staying, but lest he should go. Stopping in my writing, I lifted my left hand from the paper, stretched it out to the pile of books, and moved the top one. I cannot explain why I did this – my arm passed in front of the figure, and it vanished.

I was simply disappointed, and nothing more. I went on with my writing as if nothing had happened, perhaps for another five minutes, and had actually got to the last few words of what I had determined to extract, when the figure appeared again, exactly in the same place and attitude as before.'

Dr Jessop saw the hand close to his own and wanted to speak to the visitor, but dared not. He said that he was afraid of the sound of his own voice and returned to his own writing, which upon later examination showed no signs of tremor or nervousness.

'Having finished my task, I shut the book and threw it on the table. It made a slight noise as it fell, and the figure vanished. Throwing myself back in my chair, I sat for some seconds looking at the fire, with a curious mixture of feeling, and I remember wondering whether my friend would come again, and, if he did, whether he would hide the fire from me. Then first there stole upon me a dread and a suspicion that I was beginning to lose my nerve.'

Dr Jessop replaced the books on their shelves, with the exception of the one he had been using when the visitor appeared. He laid this one on the table.

'By this time I had lost all sense of uneasiness. I blew out all the candles and marched off to bed, when I slept the sleep of the just – or the guilty, I know not which, but I slept very soundly. And this is the conclusion of the story; but whether hallucination, spectral illusion, or trickery, no one has been able to prove, and as the hero of the tale declines to proffer explanation, theory or inference, the affair continues to be a mystery.'

Later a steward confided that the only 'ghost' seen by Dr Jessop was that of a hale and hearty servant who had come in to remove the brandy bottle. However, the antiquarian denied the man's aspersion that he was drunk. He had only been drinking seltzer.

This well documented incident remains a mystery, especially as Dr Augustus Jessop appears to be the only person to have seen 'The Mannington Ghost'.

NORTH WALSHAM

Déjà Vu!

THE gist of this chilling anecdote appeared in *Norfolk and Norwich Notes and Queries* on 13th February 1897. It concerned a strange local occurrence and was taken from *An Essay on the Science of Acting*.

In 1788 the play *The Fair Penitent* was produced in North Walsham. In the last act the character Calista has to lay her head on a skull. The actress Mrs Barry gave a good performance, but felt terribly ill when her head touched the skull. She turned pale, then crashed onto the stage in a dead faint. The woman was unwell for the rest of that night, but her condition had improved by the next morning. She was then sufficiently strong to send for the stage-keeper, to quiz him about the skull.

'Where had he got it?' she asked.

'From the sexton.'

'Whose remains were they?'

'Those of an actor,' he replied.

'What was his name?'

'Mr Norris.'

'Was he sure the name was Norris?'

'Positive. He had been buried twelve years in St Nicholas's graveyard.'

Poor Mrs Barry gave a loud shriek, turned the colour of porridge and went back into shock. Within six weeks she was dead. Mr Norris had been her first husband!

NORWICH

A Theatrical Ghost

THE Maddermarket Theatre stands on the western side of the Maddermarket, in the centre of the city. This is where in medieval times, people brought plants to sell. These were called 'madder', for when processed they yielded a red dye of that name. This was used by the local spinners for dyeing their cloth and is still a popular natural colouring agent.

Before its present use, the building, which is dated 1794, was used variously as a Catholic chapel, a baking powder factory and a Salvation Army citadel. It was standing empty when Mr Nugent Monck, the founder of the Maddermarket Theatre, discovered it in 1921. He pawned most of his belongings and bought the place.

Monck was a musician, actor and director, who settled in Norwich in 1911 and formed the Guild of Norwich Players. By 1921 the company was so successful that it needed a bigger venue. Over the years the theatre has been greatly extended and now houses what is reputed to be the best amateur company in the country. If past reports are correct, it used to house a ghost!

During one of Nugent Monck's many lectures, he stated that, 'Most theatres worthy of the name have a ghost.' Although he confessed to not believing in them, he reckoned he had a great capacity for seeing them. Especially the one in his new theatre. However, he was not on his own when it came to strange experiences. During a Saturday matinee in the 1920s Peter Taylor Smith, who was prompting, noticed a priest standing near him. The figure was staring at the audience, then disappeared without trace. This was also noticed by a Catholic priest who was at that performance. He claimed to have seen the vision before, kneeling in prayer one moment and vanishing the next. According to legend it was a priest whose mass had been interrupted in the distant past and who was returning to complete it.

Once Mr Monck saw the figure cross from where one confessional box used to stand, to the position of another on the far side of the theatre. One night when he returned to the building without switching on the lights, he felt 'something ghastly cold', as he stood within this area.

Poor Pat Bullen, the stage manager, certainly had a fright when he was going up to the lighting box at the back of the theatre. What appeared to be a figure in a black coat was climbing the ladder ahead of him! Pat followed it, but there was no-one in the box, which had no other exit. He too confirmed that he did not believe in ghosts. But he had to admit there were times when there was a strange feeling about the place. On the other hand, there were long stretches when everything was all right.

Percy Ayres also experienced some unpleasantness when he was doing some under-stage wiring. He said that he had definitely heard someone walking on the boards above him and called to the person to give him a hand. There was no response, so he called again to whoever it was still pacing up and down above him. Eventually he crawled out to see who the unhelpful person was and the theatre was empty.

Strange perfume was sometimes smelled by Lionel Dunn.

This was when he went into the building some Sunday mornings. He reckoned that it smelled like newly swung incense. On occasions when he was preparing something on stage, he also had the strange feeling that he was being watched from the empty auditorium.

All this happened some 70 years ago. Nowadays any supernatural, spine tingling fear is confined to the Elizabethan-style stage and received with applause. The ghosts appear to have gone to ground and hopefully will stay there.

St William of Norwich

IN the Middle Ages many pilgrims visited Norwich Cathedral to worship at the shrine of a twelve year old boy. He was St William, whom the Jews were alleged to have murdered in 1144.

At that time Norwich had a large and prosperous Jewish community. Anti-Semitic feelings were running high throughout England and the rest of Europe and often spurious tales of crimes committed by that race led to revenge and bloodshed, as happened in this city.

Fired by racial hatred, the terrible rumour spread that at every Passover, the Jews were obliged to murder a Christian boy child. He was a symbol of Jesus Christ, whom they had rejected and his death was one step forward to them regaining the Promised Land. It was said lots were drawn amongst their world leaders, who met in France, to determine which country and community was to provide the victim and kill him. In 1144 it was the turn of England and Norwich.

William was apprenticed to a local skinner. Shortly before Easter of that year, he was said to have been enticed into a house where a large number of Jews were assembled. At first he was treated with kindness, then tortured in a variety of ways.

His body was concealed in a sack and taken on Good Friday for burial in Thorpe Wood, close by the city. However, the Jews were seen by a local man. This was Aelward Ded who, becoming suspicious of the contents of the sack, touched it. He was convinced that it contained a human body. The men fled

71

deeper into the wood and hung their burden on a tree, then returned to Norwich and confessed their crime to the sheriff, John de Caineto. He was bribed with 100 marks to keep quiet and Ded was taken to the castle and forced to sign an oath that he would not divulge what he had seen.

The body was found by Henry de Sprowston, a forester, and later identified as being William, the son of farmer Wenstan and his wife Elviva. Crowds came to look at the corpse, which was buried on Easter Monday at the place where it had been found. A few days later the family had the body exhumed.

It was interred in holy ground and the leaders of the Jewish community were accused of murdering the child. The Bishop sent out a summons for them to appear before him, but the sheriff gave them sanctuary in the castle. Eventually, when King Stephen visited Norwich, he adjourned the case brought against the Jews for ritual murder and it never came to court. However, a large number suffered at the hands of the Norwich citizens.

Sometime later a visiting prior asked to take William's remains back with him to Sussex. The body was exhumed again and showed no signs of decay. The city decided it had a saint on its hands and on 24th April 1144 the holy relics were removed to the cathedral precincts and interred in the monks' cemetery. Not all the monks accepted the new cult, but miracles are said to have occurred. One was of a virgin who was plagued by the Devil disguised as a handsome young man. She was told in a vision to pray at William's grave and immediately the man lost interest in her!

Nine years later the holy relics were transferred to the Chapter House and later still to a shrine placed near the high altar in the cathedral. Pilgrims flocked to witness even greater wonders performed by St William. These included a certain monk recovering the power of sleeping; sailors on the sea were delivered from peril; a poor woman's hog was cured and oxen stricken with the plague were restored to health. The saint himself manifested in a vision his desire that his tomb be kept clean and carefully guarded. A sorceress was repelled from the altar and many other fantastic events were said to have been brought about.

So many people visited the shrine that on 5th April 1154

it was removed to the Jesus Chapel, then dedicated to the Holy Martyrs. William's story was recorded by Thomas of Monmouth, a monk of the Benedictine priory, who between 1172–73 wrote a lengthy 'history' of the child who became a saint. This inflamed terrible passions, leading to the persecution of many innocent Jewish people. Large numbers vanished from the city, others 'perished by the visitation of sudden death'.

The shrine remained until the Reformation, by which time the saint's appeal was waning. All that is left is a small lump of stone to mark the place and commemorate man's inhumanity to man.

OLD HUNSTANTON

The Curse of the Persian Carpet

THE late 15th century moated Hunstanton Hall has survived two bad fires and is now converted into flats. For many centuries it was the home of the le Strange family, whose ancestor Roland le Strange came over from France in 1100. The head of the family is always the Hereditary Lord High Admiral of the Wash. He/she can claim possession of anything on the beach or in the sea, as far as a man can ride a horse or throw a spear.

The spectre of Dame Armine le Strange is still claimed to be seen in parts of Old Hunstanton, disguised as 'The Grey Lady'.

Armine married into the wealthy Styleman family from Snettisham. They lived at Old Hall, the William and Mary residence next to the parish church. This became her home until her brother Sir Henry died without issue. She was his successor and returned to Hunstanton Hall, now a widow and accustomed to grief. The Stylemans had four sons, but only Nicholas survived and he subsequently took the name of le Strange. He was better known locally as 'The Jolly Gentleman', who gambled away much of the family fortune in an effort to pay off his debts.

A portrait painted of Armine in her middle years, hung in the drawing room alongside the other family likenesses. However, this grey-haired woman was said to follow you with her eyes. It was almost as if she were alive within its frame.

If Nicholas's passion was for the good life, his mother's was her old Persian carpet, which incorporated an ancient and mysterious poem in its design. It was belived to have been a gift from the Shah of Persia and mercifully had not fallen prey to her spendthrift son. We are told that as Armine lay dying, she made The Jolly Gentleman swear a binding oath concerning her beloved possession. He gave his word that neither he nor his descendants would despoil or remove it from the hall. The mistress of Old Hunstanton swore that if his pledge was broken, she would return and haunt the house. After her funeral the carpet was removed from the drawing room, nailed securely in a wooden box and put in the attic.

The new heir died in 1788, and was buried at St Mary's, Snettisham. The Persian carpet lay forgotten in the dusty roof space for another 80 years and the old lady rested peacefully. When Hamon le Strange inherited the hall, his bride Emmeline came across the box when she explored her new home. She ordered the lid to be opened and was disappointed to find just a musty old carpet, unfit for use.

Being of a thrifty nature, she is alleged to have cut it into hearthrugs and personally delivered them to the needy. On her return up the drive at dusk, she happened to glance up at the first floor. A woman was glaring down at her from one of the windows. Despite her evil expression, the stranger looked vaguely familiar. Before she reached the front door, Emmeline le Strange was convinced the face was identical to Dame Armine's ominous grey-haired portrait.

Sir Hamon was informed and this jogged his memory regarding the curse of the Persian carpet. He insisted that all the pieces be returned to their rightful place. His wife was dismissive, even though from that night on, her furious ancestor glided about the hall. She became 'The Grey Lady', the terror of Old Hunstanton. Eventually the rugs were collected and returned to the hall, in an attempt to lay the ghost. Armine was not fooled. Her carpet was ruined.

And they say that she haunted remorselessly all the time her descendants lived at Hunstanton Hall. Occasionally she is still seen drifting about the place. Only a very short time ago a woman 'all dressed in grey with long floating grey hair' was seen outside the parish church.

QUIDENHAM

The Ghostly Funeral Party

THE so called 'demon drink' is a popular subject for legends. We are told that a certain bibulous Lord Albemarle of Quidenham Hall, took things a bit too far when he made plans for his burial. Of course many people request their favourite hymns and Bible readings, but his lordship was alleged to have been unconcerned about what happened in church. His priority was the style in which he arrived. Booze was his passion and he ordered himself a truly alcoholic funeral procession. Unfortunately we are not told when this occurred.

He instructed that when he died, his coffin was to be carried to his grave by twelve drunken men. This had to be done as the clock struck midnight. Tradition states that his wishes were honoured. Unfortunately when the intoxicated pall-bearers came to the bridge near the churchyard, they and their burden tumbled into the river. On certain nights the incident is re-enacted. You can hear the faltering steps of the now ghostly procession, walking through the village. Ribald songs and raucous laughter fill the air, until the group reach the river. Now the singing stops. There is an almighty splashing sound, followed by terrible curses and the sound of drowning men.

The reputed experience of the fourth Earl of Albemarle adds a flourish to the tale. Somebody tipped him off that a gang of poachers was planning to raid his pheasants. The earl decided to ambush them some 60 yards below the infamous bridge. He and his keepers were claimed to have been badly shocked, not by the thieves, who were soon forgotten, but it was what they saw and heard which scared the life out of them. First came the sound of horses and the rumbling of wheels coming from a distance. Then a hearse could be seen, drawn by four large horses and driven by a headless horseman, crossing the old bridge.

Needless to say, the supernatural perambulations have been erased from memory and the mainly Georgian Quidenham Hall is now a Carmelite monastery. It stands eleven miles north-east of Thetford.

RANWORTH

The Wicked Colonel

THE 'Queen of the Broads' lies some four miles north-west of Acle. The approach to the 17th century Old Hall is to the left of the hill leading from the broad to the church. According to tradition this drive is haunted each year by the terrible spectre of a one-time owner, Colonel Sir Thomas Sidley. It happens on the last day of December, the anniversary of when this squire of Ranworth paid his dues to the Devil.

Amongst other things, he was said to be a cruel debauched Sabbath breaker. He was also a great huntsman, who usually outrode the rest of the hunt at such a pace that his poor mount died under him. Sidley boasted that he could ride like the Devil incarnate and often a mysterious man dressed in black was seen galloping by his side. However, enquiries as to his identity always brought his standard reply, 'Go to Hell!' Apparently the stranger was invisible to Sir Thomas.

We are told that on the 31st December 1770, a meet was held at the Old Hall. This was the high spot of the season, with a hunt ball to follow later that night. The huntsmen broke for lunch at The Rising Sun at Coltishall, where the squire had too much to drink. He challenged one of the riders to a race to Hoveton St John. The dare was accepted. In time Sidley realised that he was in danger of losing and not being a man to lose, he shot the horse in front. It fell mortally wounded. Its rider sustained fatal injuries and was left to die alongside the animal whilst his murderer rode back victorious.

That night, halfway through the ball, a footman announced that there was a stranger outside. He wished to see the master, who reacted with his customary, 'Tell him to go to Hell!' The doors were immediately flung open and in marched the tall skeleton of a man. He was dressed in dark robes, his face half concealed by a black hood. With an amazing strength he grasped the squire by the throat and ran out into the darkness with him. The most terrible stench of burning brimstone was left in their wake.

The merry-makers raced outside. They watched the Devil fling the screaming man over the saddle of his great black charger. Then he galloped off with his prisoner towards the Broad and over the mere. His horse's hooves caused steam to rise each time they touched the water.

The Wicked Colonel was never seen alive again, but for many years a strange occurrence was alleged to take place at Ranworth. On the anniversary of Sir Thomas Sidley's dreadful disappearance a huge black horse with red-hot hooves raced down the drive of Old Hall. It was ridden by a dark cloaked stranger, holding a struggling man. The animal bolted off down the hill and over the water, scattering steam and spray in all directions. People said it was the Devil and Sir Thomas. They were going to Hell.

REEDHAM

St Edmund, King and Martyr

EDMUND, who claimed his kingdom of East Anglia after coming ashore at Hunstanton, is thought to have been killed by Danish invaders at Hoxne, Suffolk, in AD 870. His death was alleged to have been caused by the lies of his friend.

It is said that in AD 866 the king's court was held at Reedham, six miles south of Acle. At that same time a Danish nobleman of great strength was out hawking along the west Danish coast. He was Ragnar Lodbrok, also known as 'Hairy-breeches' because of his clothing. A violent storm brewed up and blew his boat across the North Sea. It ended up at the mouth of the river Yare, which was then at Caister. Lodbrok sailed up the river to Reedham, where he landed and was well received by the young king. Because of his nationality, the monarch was compelled to treat him as a prisoner, but gave him many privileges.

The Dane became a good friend of Berne, the king's chief huntsman, who subsequently grew jealous of the other's skills. He killed him and hid his body in the woods. Search parties scoured the area without success, looking for the missing prisoner. It was noticed that his little dog, who returned regularly to be fed, always dashed back to the woods. He guarded one spot in particular and often scratched at the earth. Soon the body was exhumed and Berne confessed to the crime. As a punishment he was placed in his victim's boat without food, sails, oars or rudder, then taken out to sea.

A south-west wind sprang up and blew him to the Danish coast. His craft was recognised as that belonging to Lodbrok 'Hairy-breeches'. Berne the huntsman eventually confessed to his crime, but claimed to have been carrying out King Edmund's orders. He was executed and the Danes retaliated.

Lodbrok's two sons, Ubba and Hinvar the Boneless, were said to have headed an invasion of some 2,000 Danes to avenge their father's death. They sailed to England later that year, landing in East Anglia and plundering most of that region. Edmund put up a good fight, but was finally overwhelmed at Hoxne and taken prisoner. He was given a choice. His life would be spared if he denied Christ and honoured the Danes. The monarch refused the terms and replied:

'Stained as ye are with the blood of my people, ye deserve the punishment of death; but following the example of Christ, I will not pollute my hands with your blood. Go back to your masters and tell them, though they may rob me of wealth and my kingdom, which Divine Providence has bestowed upon me, they shall not make me subject to infidels. After slaying the servants slay the king, whom the King of Kings will translate into heaven, there to reign forever.'

Torture and martyrdom followed. First he was scourged, then tied to an oak tree as a target for the Danish archers. His body was so full of arrows that a chronicler of the time likened him to a hedgehog. The ordeal ended with decapitation. The Danes took his severed head and body into the thickest part of the woods at Eglesdene, near Hoxne.

The legend continues that after the enemy had retreated, some of the king's men came to retrieve his body. They found it still tied to the tree, but the head could not be found. Search parties went deeper into the dense forest, often calling to each other, 'Where are you? Where are you?' Suddenly they heard a voice coming from some way off saying, 'Here! Here! Here!' There was the head, lying in a thicket of thorns, between the front paws of a large guardian wolf. The animal willingly surrendered its 'treasure', which was taken to lie beside Edmund's remains. The wolf even joined the sad procession, then returned to the wood, and howled mournfully. Sometime later the king's body became miraculously intact.

Thirty years after his death, St Edmund's body was removed to a shrine in the abbey at what is now Bury St Edmunds. It was the goal of countless pilgrims, until it was stolen during King John's reign and taken to France.

An ancient oak which crashed to the ground near Hoxne in 1848 was found to have a Danish arrow embedded in its trunk. It was declared to be the very one against which the young king had been slain. A terrible end to the story which had begun in Reedham in friendship just a few years before.

SANTON DOWNHAM

The Four-Legged Ghosts

SANTON DOWNHAM lies on the borders of Norfolk and Suffolk, deep within Thetford Forest. The Forestry Commission revived this once almost dead Breckland village and is the main employer. The little church of All Saints had its nave rebuilt in 1628 and the chancel added in 1858. However, the building has fallen into disrepair on more than one occasion, so it is difficult to date this traditional tale.

At the time of a very hot harvest, a man who had been working hard in the fields for a long time became very thirsty. He told his mates that he was going down to St Helen's Well to cool down. They reminded him about the danger of drinking icy cold water in such weather, but he would not listen. He drank his fill, dropped dead on the spot and his spirit haunted the area for a long time.

Several years later a local man made the seven mile journey to Thetford. He spent most of his time in his favourite inn and walked home in good spirits. When he came alongside St Helen's Well, he thought he saw the phantom water drinker. The traveller was scared witless and there being no houses nearby, rushed off and took refuge in the church. At that time its fabric was in very poor order and there was even a great hole in one of its walls. The night was dark. The building cold and creepy.

The man was a gibbering wreck when discovered the next morning. He claimed ghosts had been walking about in the pitch black church. One had even bumped into him! Then the church bell had started tolling and sounded like a death knell. It took an age for him to recover from his ordeal, and even longer to accept the truth. Some sheep had crawled in through the hole. There were more of them wandering about All Saints than there were people in the Sunday congregation! As for the death knell, one of the animals had got caught up in the bell rope and was trying to get free. These were definitely strange ghosts for the sober, but surely frightening for the drunk!

St Helen's Well is really a spring, which still bubbles under the Thetford to Brandon railway bridge, about half a mile beyond the church. It has been suggested that an earlier church, maybe dedicated to St Helen, stood close to this spot but there are no records to support this.

SHERINGHAM

Give Us Strength!

SHERINGHAM is one of the 'Poppyland' seaside resorts. 'Poppyland' was born from the sentimental writing of the journalist Clement Scott, who first visited the area in 1883. The new railway brought thousands of visitors to see the great swathes of red flowers which formed the basis of his popular essays and poems. A thriving industry capitalised on this natural asset, but by 1912 it was no longer the prime attraction to the Norfolk coast.

The town lies four miles west of Cromer and is noted for its crabs. In days past the Sheringham and Cromer crabbers were sworn enemies and often engaged in pub brawls. However, the proverb 'It's an ill wind that blows nobody any good', proved to be true in 1928. This was when a Sheringham boat, which was out whelking, got caught in a terrible storm. At that time the town did not own a motor lifeboat. Just as the boat was going down, a man from the Cromer lifeboat jumped aboard and managed to save most of its crew. They say that since that time the two towns have more or less been friends!

The cuts and bruises brought about by this local rivalry were small beer, compared with the threat which hung over the Sheringhammers back in the 17th century. At that time they felt extremely vulnerable to attack by the Dutch privateers often seen sailing off the coast. In 1673 this fear reached its climax. The Lord Lieutenant and his deputies were petitioned to safeguard their welfare.

'Our Town Joynes upon ye Maine sea and we are afraid every night ye enemy should come ashore and fire Our Towne when we be in our Bedds; for ye Houses stand close together, and all ye houses Thatched with straw, that in one houres time ye towne may be burnt, for we have nothing to Resist them but one Gunn with a broken carriage and foure Musquetts which we bought at Our Owne cost and charges; which is a small defence against an enemy; and likewise wee have no pouder nor shot for ye said Gunn, nor Musquetts, when wee stand in need. Wee Therefore humbly beseech your Honrs yt you would be pleased to consider ye danger wee live in, and that your Honrs would grant us foure or five Musquetts more, and half a hundred pound of powder and half a hundred pound of Bullet; and wee should think wee were able to defend ye attempt of a Dutch privateer.'

Their request was granted. Six new muskets and the required amount of ammunition were added to their arsenal. However, the gifts were dependent upon the defenders of Sheringham not to 'imbocill ye said arms and amunition'!

When the Yow-Yows Call

BEFORE the railway came to Sheringham and made it a popular seaside resort, its main occupation was fishing. Most fishermen were superstitious and many claimed to hear the Yow-Yows or ghostly sailors, wailing from a spot not far off the coast. It was said that a shipful of mariners had drowned there a long time ago. Lives could have been saved, but the fishermen of the day turned their backs on them. And they still yelled for help on occasions!

Some were fooled into thinking these were genuine cries of distress, and went to give help. When they reached the source of the noise, the pitiful cries immediately changed direction, as if playing tricks. However, it was more common for people to haul in their nets and make haste for the safety of the shore and their flint cottages. A terrible storm was never far behind the call of the Yow-Yows.

These invisible phantoms have kept their silence for many years, the Met Office weather forecasts being more reliable.

SOUTHWOOD

The Treasure of Callow Pit

SOME people connect the pit to the west side of the junction between Southwood and Moulton at OS map 134 TG394058 with the 'Treasure of Callow Pit'. I was told this by a farmer whose family has long connections with the Halvergate Marshes. Long ago people claimed a headless horseman rode close to this isolated place. The pit was also rumoured to be used by a gang of local smugglers for hiding their booty. However, according to legend, something far more exciting lay within its muddy depths – an iron chest filled with gold.

Ages ago, two daring men tried to get it out. When the water was suitably low, long ladders were placed across the hole to form a temporary bridge. They fished about with a sturdy staff and used the thick iron hook at one end to catch hold of the ring on the lid of the chest. With much difficulty the casket was heaved onto the bridge. The adventurers then pushed the staff through the ring in readiness for carrying it away. Luck was on their side! Or was it?

There has always been the belief that when meddling with the Devil or the supernatural, silence is essential for success. However, one of the men was so elated by his promised wealth that he shouted, 'We've got it safe and Old Nick himself can't get it from us!' The pit was immediately engulfed in a sulphuric vapour. The Devil's black hand came up through the water and grabbed hold of the precious chest.

A desperate struggle ensued between the two men and the Prince of Darkness. During the jostling the chest fell away from the ring and sank to the bottom of the water. The thieves were left with just the iron circlet still threaded through their staff. With nothing to show for their trouble, they fixed it to the door of Southwood church. This building was made redundant in the late 19th century and is now a ruin. The ring is thought to have been transferred to the door of St Botolph's at Limpenhoe nearby, but the treasure of Callow Pit has been lost forever.

STOW BARDOLPH

The Ghost of The Hare Arms

THE Hare family has played an important role in their neighbourhood ever since Sir Nicholas Hare, Master of the Rolls and Keeper of the Great Seal, bought the freedom of the Hundred of Clackclose in 1553.

The Hare Arms has a ghost story with a difference. The sole character was said to have gone mad after eating an unsuitable pie! This was a long time ago. Since then the place has been awarded acclaimed star rating and its food is always correctly prepared!

The inn stands on a slight rise leading to the church, about two miles north-east of Downham Market. The building was erected during the Napoleonic Wars and converted into an hostelry when offered by Captain Leigh-Hare to three soldiers. Two had French surnames, Capon and Gammonier. There are no further details about these new owners. However, Capon's nasty experience with his dinner reputedly turned him into a ghost.

The story says that his wife cooked the beastly pie, and whatever she put in the filling sent him crazy. This must have reinforced the English mistrust of foreign food! Poor Capon had barely wiped the gravy from his mouth, before racing off to the coach house where he hanged himself. Allegedly it is he who still makes strange noises and causes mischief from time to time about the place. Some recent examples of his spectral activity include the crystal vase which shattered by itself in a front bedroom. Then there are footsteps often heard on the stairs leading from the bar when there is nobody about.

Mr Pat Palmer, the manager of the inn, told me of the occasion when he was relaxing in his sitting room. He had a cup of tea placed by his feet. Suddenly he had the sensation that some invisible person was walking across the room. His tea shook in confirmation. Not so long ago he was working in his first floor office above the bar. A clear voice from behind enquired, 'Are y' awright bor?' However, there was no sign of anyone who could have made this traditional Norfolk greeting.

Capon's ghost remains invisible, but many have heard it. They also blame it for the inevitable electrical breakdowns which occur when the owners of The Hare Arms are absent for any length of time. Surely this phantom deserves our sympathy. Death through possible food poisoning is a tragedy. However, to perish from a pie with qualities to create madness and an unquiet afterlife is really drawing the short straw!

The Wax Maiden

A MAHOGANY Cabinet stands in the Hare Chapel of Holy Trinity church. Open the door, for it is not locked, and be prepared for a surprise. The life-sized wax effigy of Sarah Hare peers from behind the glass front. Her eyes are bright blue and very stern. Time has made her 'skin' look like Stilton cheese soaked in port wine and she is wearing a red dress. The image is said to stand as a grim reminder to all who would labour on the Lord's Day of Rest. Sarah is believed to have died from blood poisoning, after pricking her finger whilst sewing on the Sabbath. It happened in 1744.

She was the youngest daughter of Sir Thomas Hare and in her will dated 10th August 1743 she requested:

'I desire Six of the poor men in the parish of Stow or Wimbotsham may put me in to the ground they having five shillings a piece for the same. I desire all the poor in the Alms Row may have two shillings and sixpence each person at the Grave before I am put in. This I hope my Executor will see firstly performed before sunset . . . .

I desire to have my face and hands made in wax with a piece of Crimson satin thrown like a garment in a picture, hair upon my head and put in a case of Mahogany with a glass before and fix'd up so near the place where my corpse lyes as it can be with my name and time of Death put upon the case in any manner most desirable if I do not execute this in my life I desire it may be done after my Death.'

The directions of the will were carried out to the letter. According to the pamphlet *The Saving of Sarah Hare*, this effigy is the only one of its kind known to be surviving outside those in Westminster Abbey. It is also the latest example in date of the custom of making such funerary effigies in England.

SWAFFHAM

The Swaffham Pedlar

THIS attractive market town is about 14 miles south-east of King's Lynn and has a very fine medieval church. This was built for the most part between 1454 and 1490, on the remains of the old church which had partially collapsed. According to legend the new works were mainly funded by John Chapman. He was said to be just a humble Swaffham pedlar, until he followed his dreams!

On three successive nights he dreamed that he should go to London Bridge, where he would hear something to his advantage. He took no notice, but could not rid his mind of the thought. Eventually he decided to make this arduous journey on foot, taking his dog for company. He stood as directed for many hours on the bridge, in the hope of seeing something marvellous. However, nothing materialised. He told himself that he was foolish for acting so impulsively. Just as the pedlar was about to leave for home, a shopkeeper came out and asked him what he was doing. Without mentioning his name or address, Chapman narrated his tale.

His companion chided him and said, 'Alas, good friend, if I had heeded dreams, I might have proved myself as very a fool as thou art, for 'tis not long since I dreamed that at a place called Swaffham in Norfolk dwelt John Chapman, a pedlar, who hath a tree at the back of his house, under which is buried a pot of money.'

Chapman said nothing, but turned on his heels and headed

for home. He told no-one about his adventure in the capital, but commenced digging under a large tree in his garden. To his amazement he unearthed a great pot inscribed with strange words. It was crammed with gold coins. He kept his find a secret and hid the treasure and its container amongst his other brass pots in his shop.

One day a man of great learning called at the shop. He looked at the pots and picked out the special one, which Chapman said was not for sale. The stranger asked if he knew the meaning of the words written around its lid. The pedlar shook his head and was given their translation: 'Under me doth lie another much richer than I.'

That night an even deeper hole under the tree yielded up a pot double the size of the former. It was also crammed with twice as much gold. The canny man continued to keep his secrets to himself and lived as simply as ever.

The parish church dedicated to St Peter and St Paul had been in disrepair for a very long time and was now almost in ruins. The steeple had been pulled down and the rubble sold to Alys Sadeler for 16 pence. Sadly there were insufficient funds for its restoration, yet steps had to be taken to save the building. Therefore, it was decided to impose a tax upon all the citizens of Swaffham to pay for the essential work. This news was received with displeasure.

According to the legend, the pedlar knew this was the right time to dip into his treasure pots. With no mention of the source of his wealth, he provided a new north aisle and tall steeple. The humble man had rescued the church from dereliction and saved its congregation from a burdensome tax.

Its 19th century furniture has some medieval wood carvings incorporated into the clergy stalls. The one to the south has two effigies of a man with a pack on his back, under which is a chained and muzzled dog. The northern stall has two likenesses of a shopkeeper, under which is a carving of a woman who is said to be the pedlar's wife. She is looking over a shop door. These were taken from the family pews of John Chapman, benefactor and churchwarden of St Peter and St Paul's during its restoration. The two front facing chancel pews also have fine carvings at either end. One is of a man carrying a pack, the other of a chained and muzzled dog.

It is uncertain if Chapman was actually a pedlar or how he came about his wealth. However, his was a lovely dream, and the stuff of fireside tales.

TERRINGTON ST JOHN

The Mistletoe Tree

AS soon as she was shown round the bungalow in 1976, Anita Perks knew that it was for her. The property was built in the 1930s and in need of some modernisation. However, it had a good feel about it and was ideally located halfway between Wisbech and King's Lynn. It was a case of love at first sight for this little dwelling, which was to become associated with the supernatural.

Mrs Perks says there was one thing which she did not like. This was the strange, sickly sweet smell which permeated the building. It was especially strong in the kitchen. However, she reasoned that new paint and some fresh air should put that right. The purchase was completed, the renovations were undertaken, but still the smell remained. Floorboards were checked and drains re-inspected. The source of the odour could not be traced, although over the months it slowly faded away.

The family registered with the local doctor. When he saw their address, he said in passing that presumably he would have to forego his usual Christmas mistletoe. Apparently the previous owner X, now deceased, had always given him a bunch from his garden. Anita assured him she would not break with tradition.

Over the months she learned how X had grafted a couple of mistletoe berries onto the apple tree many years ago. They grew into a large clump of green and white which fed the greedy mistle thrushes. Apparently the old Fenman had strong feelings for this plant which he had helped create. In his later years he would go out and stand beside it, maybe several times a day.

He would stare at it, thinking his private thoughts. It became his place of quiet meditation. Everyone who knew him said there was no doubt that X was proud of his mistletoe. They knew better than to ask for a bunch at Christmas! However, for some reason he always cut one for the doctor.

The old man had lived close to the land and rarely left the village. When his wife became ill and was taken to the hospital at King's Lynn, he hardly knew how to reach her. Quite possibly he had never travelled further than Sunday school outings to Hunstanton. They were a close, affectionate couple and after her funeral the sad widower went home, pulled up his favourite chair next to the kitchen range and slowly pined away. He was always to be found there and this is where he died, two years after his wife. He was seated within view of the gnarled apple tree and its verdant clump of mistletoe. By coincidence Anita felt happiest in this room, which happened to be the last to retain the smell.

Anita's mother kept a public house in Wisbech. Christmas was coming, so she cut a big bunch of mistletoe to go with the other promised greenery. The van was loaded and she set off for Wisbech. However, as she approached the doctor's surgery the all too familiar smell suddenly pervaded the vehicle. It was so sickly it made her want to gag. She immediately thought of her promise made to the GP almost a year ago. The old man seemed to be reminding her about his beloved mistletoe. Straight away Anita parked in the surgery car park and divided her bunch. Half for the doctor, which she dropped off at reception, and half for her mother. The odour immediately left the van.

Was this merely a subconscious association between the old smell and a forgotten promise? Or could this have been X's method of communication, both indoors and out? Whatever the cause, the smell did not return as long as Anita lived in the bungalow and took her Yuletide gift to the doctor.

THETFORD

Castle Hill

NOW the capital of Breckland, this was once one of the most important towns of East Anglia. Some of the bloodiest battles with the Danes were fought in the area.

There are several legends associated with the huge undated Castle Hill, which lies close to the A1066 Diss road. This is thought to be the remains of an Iron Age fort and once measured 100 ft up the slope, with a base circumference of nearly 80 ft. It was probably built to guard the point where the Icknield Way crossed the river at Nun's Bridges. In the 11th century a castle was built within its banks and ditches.

According to tradition the hill was once the site of a magnificent castle, where a powerful king stored his great hoard of treasure. During an invasion he was worried the enemy would steal his wealth. He decided to camouflage the place and fool the intruders. Hundreds of his strongest men were ordered to cart earth and throw it over the castle. The labourers did a good job and made it look like a lumpy mound. This is how we see the place today!

Another story concerning treasure tells us that at the time of the Dissolution, six silver bells were taken from Thetford Priory and hidden for safe-keeping under Castle Hill.

Some say that the Devil made these hills when he scraped his boots clean, after making the Devil's Ditch on Garboldisham Heath. He did this by dragging his foot along the ground and there was a lot of cleaning up to do afterwards. A hollow which fills with water north-east of the northern rampart is known as the Devil's Hole. They say that if you are foolish enough to walk around it seven times at midnight, you will see the evil one himself!

The Bell Hotel Ghost

THE BELL is situated in King Street and dates from 1493. It was once a coaching and posting house on the London to Norwich route. Mrs Betty Radcliffe is said to have been the owner a long time ago, although there is no recorded date. According to the tale she preferred to make her home in what is now the Ancient House Museum. This is situated in White Hart Street and only a few yards from The Bell.

Betty is still claimed to visit what is now room 10 at the Bell. This is where she once kept secret lovers' trysts with her husband's ostler. In time the man grew tired of her and wanted to end their relationship. The landlady refused and so he murdered her in the now haunted room. Mrs Radcliffe is reputed to be buried in St Peter's churchyard, which happens to be the view from room 10.

Many guests have alleged uncomfortable experiences in this bedroom. However, before I was taken to view it, I first met Mr David Govan, the manager. We were joined by Mr Fred Gurney, his predecessor, who retired several years ago. Fred said that he was first aware of ghosts a few months after his appointment in 1958. This was when a visitor refused the offer of the room, even though it was the best in the hotel and the only one vacant at that time. The man said he was aware of its reputation and would not accept it, even if it were offered free of charge!

Fred admitted that he had taken all this ghostly business with a pinch of salt, until the hotel underwent major alterations in 1964. At that time he and his wife had to constantly change bedrooms. Their dog Janey had never been any trouble, until they tried to get her to stay with them in what is now room 10. The docile animal absolutely refused to cross the threshold but would stand for hours whimpering outside the shut door. Dogs are said to be very susceptible to the supernatural and this one was greatly disturbed. It made the Gurneys wonder if there was any truth in the old tales after all.

Over the years several occupants have reported feeling ill at ease or claimed weird happenings. I was told that one man phoned down to reception at 1 am to see if he could swop accommodation. He said his wife was overcome with inexplicable terror. However, it has to be said that these 'supernatural' complaints are a minority. Many guests book room 10 on their return visits.

The present manager mentioned that his housekeeper, Terry

Carter, had a bad experience in 1992. She confirmed that it had happened after she and her assistant had finished attending the room. They were about to leave when she said in a jocular fashion, 'Well Betty, I hope you're not going to frighten any more of our customers!' Immediately both women were overcome with a bitterly cold feeling which cut right through their bodies. They exclaimed in unison, 'Did you feel that?' and raced down stairs as white as sheets.

Chambermaids have also reported nasty experiences. One had a scare after she had made the bed and went to clean the en suite bathroom. When she returned to the bedroom a few minutes later there was a dent in the bed covers. It looked as if someone had been lying on it, but the door was locked. Another woman reported leaving her large bunch of keys in the lock and said they twirled round twice all by themselves.

After more chilling tales, Fred Gurney volunteered to take me up to see the place, which he had not visited for a long time. It is also known as the 'Honeymoon Suite', because of its romantic bed. Reason told me that as this was part of a well known hotel chain, I was unlikely to encounter spiders' webs and roosting bats. However, at best, surely a 'haunted room' should feel a touch unpleasant? I prepared myself for whatever might be brooding along the sloping corridor!

On the contrary, this room has a welcoming atmosphere and is very relaxing. One's eyes are drawn immediately to the magnificent four poster bed, then to the fine 17th century mural over the massive fireplace. The painting is protected by a glass cover which is fixed firmly to the wall. To be truthful I was just as interested in this as I was in the work of art. Did it or did it not have dirty fingermarks on its reverse side? If it did, Betty Radcliffe could be about! They say she sometimes gets behind that piece of glass, despite it almost touching the wall.

The assistant curator of the Ancient House Museum had told me a chilling tale concerning this on my last visit to Thetford. He said that some two years previously a distraught looking couple had come into the museum. They asked if he knew the history of the hotel and explained that they were off home, having foreshortened their honeymoon in room 10 at The Bell. Both had come to the conclusion that it was haunted, and recounted their experience.

Despite it being their first night as man and wife, the occasion had been marred by a bad atmosphere in the room. It was nothing personal, just something in the air. The next morning they noticed several handprints on the reverse side of the mural glass. They said they found this puzzling, for the cover had been perfectly clean when they went to bed. It was impossible to touch it from the underside and a major task to remove it from the wall.

On the second night, and despite the central heating, the honeymooners had felt desperately cold in bed. Suddenly the blankets were slowly drawn away, as if by an invisible person. They did not give up, but spent the rest of the night feeling chilly and anxious. The next morning there were lots more dirty handprints on the wrong side of the glass. This was the last straw, so they settled their bill and left.

Fred Gurney told me that psychic tests have been conducted, but no conclusive evidence of the supernatural has been found. If the ghost has an existence, maybe she is unhappy with others using her old love nest. Of course the place has changed a lot since her time, whenever that was. She and the ostler could never have shared that four poster bed. However, the mural might have witnessed their passion and her murder. From within the room's comfortable old fashioned ambience, you can certainly mull over the legend and imagine Betty Radcliffe in love and death and maybe even beyond.

TILNEY ALL SAINTS

The Giant Hickathrift

TOM HICKATHRIFT, the famous legendary Marshland giant, is said to be buried in Tilney All Saints churchyard, about five miles south-west of King's Lynn. His 'grave' lies adjacent to the path by the eastern wall of the church, and alongside some iron railings. It has no marker and looks more like an 8 ft long broken drainpipe.

His story was first published in about 1790 and is set around the time of the Norman invasion. He was born at Marshland St James in the Isle of Ely, some six miles north-east of Wisbech. Tom performed many heroic feats, and was often assisted by his best friend, the tinker Henry Nonsuch. However, this hero started life as a bad lot.

The tale says he was the lazy ne'er do well son of a poor widow. At the age of ten he was 6 ft tall and 3 ft thick, with hands like shoulders of mutton. However, none were aware of his great strength, because he spent most of his time asleep in the chimney corner. His life changed when a farmer offered his mother some straw with which to stuff her mattresses. The good man said she could have as much as her idle son could carry. Tom refused, but after a lot of nagging went, and carried a whole field-full home on his back.

Soon everyone wanted to hire his services because he was so strong, but the boy still preferred the warm fire. However, the legend tells us that finally a brewer from Lynn managed to bribe him with a new suit of clothes and all the food he could eat. Tom agreed to cart his beer from Lynn to Wisbech, which was a journey of some 20 miles. There was a short cut across the Smeeth, but a warring giant guarded this huge tract of waste land. None dared pass his way, because they claimed that he either ate all trespassers or made them his slaves.

It was not long before the short cut proved too tempting for Master Hickathrift. The brute was soon upon him, demanding battle. Tom had no weapons, but swiftly upended the cart and removed its axle-tree, which he used for a staff. His shield was a cart wheel. It was not long before he had the giant on the ground, pleading for his life, but the lad had no mercy. He sliced off this villain's head, then raced back to tell his master the news. The next day most of Lynn came to see the dead giant and rejoiced at Tom's bravery. He was given the great quantity of treasure found hoarded in the tyrant's cave. He was also given the Smeeth.

Tom built a fine house for himself and his mother and turned the giant's land into common grazing pasture. It remained as such until the enclosures and is still called 'Marshland Smeeth'.

He also built a church which was dedicated to St James, for it was on that saint's day that he killed the guardian of the Smeeth. By now Tom had grown in stature as well as importance. He himself was as big as a giant and treated with respect.

One day he met a tinker called Henry Nonsuch who was trespassing on his estate. After a few heated words they had a fight. Eventually Tom was beaten by the stranger who was almost his equal in size. They became boon companions and had many adventures righting wrongs and quelling uprisings. The king bestowed a knighthood on Mr Hickathrift and a pension of 40 shillings a year on the tinker. Tom's saddest fight followed soon after his marriage to a rich widow from Cambridge. The king summoned him to the Isle of Thanet where a giant was terrorising its people. This miscreant had a Cyclops eye and hair the texture of rusty wire which hung down like coils of snakes. He rode a dragon, accompanied by a troupe of angry lions and bears. Sir Thomas went alone and felled the giant and most of his entourage. Henry joined him later to flush out the last few remaining animals and was killed. Hickathrift was devastated and when he returned home, vowed to his people to uphold the peace forever.

It is said that he determined his place of burial by throwing a stone from Marshland St James. Wherever it landed would be his final resting place. It flew several miles, then dropped down on the eastern end of Tilney All Saints churchyard. This is where he lies today, tangled with grass in the summer. His 'candlestick', which is probably part of an old memorial or preaching cross, stands opposite the south door of the church.

The giant appears on the village signs of both Marshland St James and Tilney All Saints. He also has other legendary connections with their neighbouring villages. Another 'candle-stick' is placed in the vicarage garden, close to the north door of the church at Terrington St John.

The small effigy sited on the outside wall of the north chancel of Walpole St Peter's may be a surviving Roman figure of Atlas, or it may be that of Tom Hickathrift. To the left of this stone carving is a round indentation. Traditionally it was made by the giant either when playing football in the churchyard, or the time he threw a stone at the Devil.

The Marshland hero is also held responsible for the detached tower of St Mary's church at West Walton. Some say he picked it up for a wager, then dropped it because it was too heavy even for him. Others hold the Devil responsible. He attempted to steal the tower because he hated the sound of its bells. In fact the church was built in this fashion during the 13th century. The undrained land of that time would have been incapable of bearing heavy loads.

It has been suggested that 'Hickathrift' could have been a Celtic sun god, his wheel and axle-tree representing the sun's rays. An alternative theory makes him a god worshipped by the Iceni tribe. Whatever his source, his is a good legend which should be treasured forever.

TUTT'S HILL

The Traitor Shepherd

A PREHISTORIC BARROW situated on the brow of a ridge off the A1088 Thetford to Euston Road at OS map 144 TF884814 is known as Tutt's Hill. It is the setting of a traditional tale similar to that of the traitor monk of St Benet's Abbey at Ludham. Treachery found a reward which was beyond even the highest expectation of the recipient.

The legend is set at a time when the Danes were yet again attacking Thetford. However, they were still unable to find a weak link in the town's defences. Several Saxons had been taken prisoner and tortured without success. No matter the pain, they would not divulge the secret route which led to the heart of the town. Then Tutt the traitor shepherd came forward and offered his services to the enemy.

He bargained long and hard and eventually secured the promise of a reward said to be beyond his wildest dreams. We are not told what this was, but it must have been worth the risk of revenge from those whom he was about to betray.

He told the insurgents how to cross the marshes and traverse an easy ford which crossed the river. This would take them to where the town was not protected by earthworks. Thetford was captured, but when Tutt went to collect his dues he was double-crossed. His only prize was to swing from the scaffold on what has since been known as Tutt's Hill.

WAXHAM

'Owd Sir Barney Brograve'

IN 1733 Thomas Brograve of Hertfordshire and father of the infamous 'Owd Sir Barney', purchased the manors of Worstead, Waxham and Horsey. The latter two were wild, wind-tossed areas, almost as untamed as its decadent owners! Only three generations were to live in the county, but they are fixed firmly in its folklore. Especially Berney Brograve. Although named after his mother Julian Berney, he is usually called 'Barney' in the local tongue. He was seven years old when his people moved to Norfolk.

The family lived in the flint-stoned Waxham Hall, 15 miles north of Great Yarmouth. Its neighbouring thatched barn is the largest tithe barn in Norfolk. Much of this small coastal hamlet, which once comprised Waxham Magna and Parva, now lies beneath the sea. Only part of Waxham Magna remains.

The young Berney was the only son and had a flamboyant father for a role model, which says much for his adult behaviour. In 1726 Thomas Brograve fought a duel in London with another Norfolk man, Henry Branthwayt. The account is contained in Charles Palmer's *Perlustration of Great Yarmouth* (1875):

'It is said that they went to the spot in the same Hackney coach quite unattended. Having divested themselves of their scarlet cloaks, and discarded their hats and wigs, they fired with pistols but without effect. They then drew their swords

97

and Branthwayt received a wound in his left breast which penetrated to his heart. Brograve then withdrew the bloody weapon, wiped it on the grass, and straightened it. Having kissed the dead body he waved his hat for the coach which had drawn up at Hyde Park Corner, and made off. These facts were desposed to by a witness, who said he was "taking the air soon after noon" on the day near the place where the duel was fought.'

Berney was claimed to be a notorious hedonist at a young age. When William Marshall, the author of *The Rural Economy of Norfolk* paid him a visit in 1782 he later wrote:

'His person is gross, his appearance Bacchanalian – his dress that of a slovenly gentleman. There is a politeness in his manner: and his conversation bespeaks a sensible intelligent mind: borne away, however, by a wildness and ferocity which is obvious in his countenance and discovers itself in every word and action.'

The terrible squire of Waxham was created a baronet in 1791. His eccentricities were known far and wide, and he was said to be never happier than when engaged in a brawl. According to legend he once insisted on fighting a sweep over payment, after the chimneys at the hall had been swept. If the man won he would receive double his asking price, which Brograve considered to be extortionate. However, if he lost, he would get nothing but a good thrashing. The sweep was the loser, but such were Sir Barney's punches that he nearly choked to death on the soot and muck which flew from the poor man's clothing. Apparently it took him a week or two of serious drinking to get the taste out of his mouth!

There are many apocryphal tales connected with this man and his relatives. For instance six members of his family were said to haunt the hall, which was not Brograve property until 1733. The ghostly visitors wined and dined with Berney every New Year's Eve. All were said to have died violently in battle. They were:

Sir Ralph who was killed in the Crusades
Sir Edmund in the Baron's Wars
Sir John at Agincourt
Sir Frances in the Wars of the Roses
Sir Thomas at Marston Moor
Sir Charles at Ramillies.

These phantom ancestors always left at the stroke of midnight, and have stayed away for a long time.

No wonder Berney Brograve was alleged to have sold his soul to the Devil. He even received a 'parchment bond' as proof of the contract! When he died he called on his satanic master, who congratulated him for being a man of his word. However 'Old Nick' confessed that he had been looking through the squire's account. It was so bad, he feared that within a short time he would be playing second fiddle to the Norfolk gentleman! He returned the contract and told him to go away. Brograve asked where he should go. Without thinking the Devil replied angrily, 'Oh, go to Hell!' so he sat down and stayed there. And they do say there are two devils there now!

The old man was succeeded by his fierce son Sir George who kept a pack of equally ferocious hounds at Waxham. Their fearful baying could be heard from miles away and scared people half to death. The family title became extinct on his death in 1828, but the Brograves are not forgotten. They have their legends and a large tract of marshland which bears their name. According to tradition, 'Owd Sir Barney' himself is seen on wild stormy nights, riding horseback between his Waxham and Worstead estates. Another of his tales is in the Worstead section.

WEYBOURNE

A Prophesy

WEYBOURNE HOPE, or Hoop, lies west of Sheringham and is reached by a road leading from the village. This is where the Danes were said to have landed during one of their many assaults on East Anglia. At that point the deep water close to the shore offered excellent anchorage for invading ships. For a long time it was believed to be the gateway to England, hence the adage:

> 'He who must old England win,
> Must at Weybourne Hoop begin.'

Therefore when the *Sundry Strange Prophecies of Merlin* were published in 1652, the following prediction would have been a terrible threat to many superstitious people.

'There shall come out of Denmark a duke; and he shall bring with him the King of Denmark and 16 great lords of his company. They shall land at 'Waborne Stone', they shall be met by the Red Deare, the Heath Cock, the Hound and the Harrow, between 'Waborne' and 'Branksbim' [Brancaster?] a Forest and a Church gate. There shall be fought so mortal a battle that from Branksbrim to Cromer Bridge it shall run blood. There the King of Denmark shall be slain and all the perilous fishes in his company. Then the Duke shall go forth to Clare Hall, where the Bare and the headless men shall meet him and slay all his Lords and take him prisoner, and send him to Blanchflower and chase his men to the sea, where twenty thousand of them shall be drowned without dint of sword.

Then shall come in the French King and he shall land at Waborne Hoop, 18 miles from Norwich; then he shall be let in by a false Mayor, and there shall he keep for his lodging a while . . . .'

Perhaps 'Merlin' foresaw the 'Red Deare' and the 'Heath Cock' etc as being armorial emblems, carried by the defenders of the coast. Thankfully his prophesy was false.

Being an island, Britain's coastal defences have always been of paramount importance, especially during periods of war. At the time of the Spanish Armada, Weybourne was well fortified against the hated 'Spannyardes'. During the First World War trenches were dug on Beeston Heath and in the Second World War troops were concentrated in this area to resist invasion. Nowadays its only 'invaders' are likely to be tourists. All are welcome, even the 'Spannyardes' and the Danes!

WICKHAMPTON

The Heart in the Hand

THIS little hamlet stands close to the Halvergate Marshes, which stretch eastwards towards Great Yarmouth. According to legend the names 'Wickhampton' and 'Halvergate' arose from a dispute over land.

Set into niches in the northern wall of the isolated St Andrew's church are the 13th century tombs with effigies of Sir William de Gerbygge and his lady. These are thought to be dated about 1270 and could be one of the earliest examples of three-dimensional effigies in a Norfolk church. The knight holds a heart in his hands, which are placed against his breast. His wife is also thought to have once held a heart. Their identity was probably long forgotten when the tale was first told, to explain why a knight should be holding his heart in his hands.

It is said that two brothers named Hampton were both masters of neighbouring parishes. They quarrelled long and hard over a boundary dispute and eventually their tempers boiled over. They fought bitterly until each tore the other's heart out. This angered the Almighty, who vowed to make them an example to all men who might be tempted into similar acts of wickedness. He put their hearts in their hands, then turned them into stone and placed them in Wickhampton church, where they remain to this day.

After the death of the brothers one parish was called Wicked Hampton, since contracted into Wickhampton. The other became Hell Fire Gate, now known as Halvergate.

WINFARTHING

The Sword of the Good Thief

THE parish church of this village near Diss once possessed a miraculous sword. Known as the 'Sword of the Good Thief', it was housed in a shrine in the former chapel of the 'Good Sword of Winfarthing'. This was placed at the eastern end of the south aisle. The weapon was believed to have originally been owned by a robber. According to legend, he had taken sanctuary in St Mary's and then escaped, leaving it behind. This became 'of so great a virtue that there was a solomne pilgrimage used unto it with large gifts and offringes, with vow makings, crouchings and kissenges.'

Its amazing powers came to light after being handled out of curiosity by a woman desperate to conceive. Shortly afterwards she became pregnant. Soon pilgrims flocked to touch the sword and pray before it, bringing money and gifts with them. It was used for purposes other than promoting fertility in barren women. Those seeking lost articles had only to touch its cold metal and they would find whatever they were seeking. This method was said to be especially good for locating strayed or stolen horses.

Any youth who came barefoot and 'made long and humble supplication then would his lady be like to look on him with favour'. It would work, even if she had previously thwarted his attentions. Devout couples presented themselves before its long glistening blade to ensure a fruitful marriage, and got results.

However, the wonderful object did have its sinister side, at least for men. It was alleged that women could easily kill their husbands by lighting a candle and placing it before the sword. This had to be done every Sunday without omission for a whole year. It was said that all efforts to help him would be in vain, 'her light becoming his extinguisher'.

Although lost during the Reformation, the 'Sword of the Good Thief' is depicted in the Cole memorial window, dedicated in 1957.

WINTERTON-ON-SEA

The Ploughman and the Fairies

A CONTRIBUTOR to the Folklore Society's *Folklore* Vol 7 1896 recorded a story narrated by a local woman, Mrs Goodale. She had been told it by her grandmother, who had died the previous year at the age of 102. I do not know if the tale was based on fact, around someone who had quickly changed from being poor to rich, or was just a yarn.

It concerned a poor labourer with a large family to support, at a time when food was dear. One day, as he was going off to plough his master's eleven acre field, he confided to his wife that he wished a good fairy would bring them some luck. He started ploughing and found a bright freshly minted shilling at the foot of the plough. He put it in his pocket, then prayed for more. The next morning he found two more coins lying on the freshly turned furrows of the previous day. He put them in his pocket and prayed for more. On the third morning there were three shillings waiting for him. When he returned home he told his wife that he was in no hurry to finish his work. The longer the field took to plough, the better it was for him.

Soon he had collected a great stack of coins and knowing that his children and woman were in need, he gave her ten shillings. She was suspicious and asked where they had come from, but he would not say. However, she took the money and bought necessities. Each day she was given more.

Unfortunately when the ploughman's wife went to the mill to buy flour, the miller demanded to know the source of the glistening shillings. She replied they were a gift from her husband. He refused them as payment, for he had heard rumours concerning this shining money.

The woman implored her man to be truthful and the miller called on him to investigate. This infuriated the ploughman who exclaimed that he could keep his flour! His wife and family would starve before he said anything! He told her that she could collect his next week's wages, but the master refused her. He too quizzed his labourer, who kept his silence and was given the sack.

With no money coming in, the family tried to pass more of the spanking new coins, which nobody would accept. Things went from bad to worse and soon they were almost starving. At last the unemployed man was forced to divulge the source of his money. He knew the fairies would be cross with him if he broke his silence. And he was right. There were no more coins in the field.

According to the teller of this tale, there were plenty in the village who would have given much to have never interfered. Then they could all have shared in the wealth of Joe the ploughman.

WIVETON

Vicars and Actresses

VICARS and actresses are in the same league as banana skins when it comes to awful jokes. However, the incumbents of two Norfolk parishes within a close distance of each other have theatrical associations. Both attracted scandal and suffered the consequences.

In the 18th century attention was fixed on Wiveton and the shocking revelations concerning their new vicar and a gorgeous actress. The Reverend James Hackman, a former soldier, was only 27 years old when he took up his living. His infatuation with Martha Reay, a staymaker's daughter, had begun a long time before then. Martha may have started life in humble circumstances, but with her good looks, a will of iron and a theatrical career, she swiftly scaled the social ladder. The fourth Earl of Sandwich made her his longstanding mistress and fathered her children.

The earl was an inveterate gambler who could not bear to leave the tables, even for a meal. He used to order the waiters to bring him a snack of ham or beef placed between two slices of bread. The idea caught on and Sandwich unwittingly became the 'patron saint' of pack-up food and finger buffets. He might have gained culinary fame, but he lost his mistress. The obsessive parson from Wiveton saw to that.

For a long time James Hackman had loved Martha from a distance, and with a vigour unsuited to a man of his future calling. But eventually even he had to admit that the beautiful woman would never be his. By now his irrational passion had grown to terrifying jealousy, which caused him to make careful plans. He travelled to London without drawing attention to himself and went to Covent Garden where Miss Reay was appearing in the aptly named play *Love in a Village*.

Like any other admirer, Hackman waited patiently by the stage door. However, he was not holding flowers, just a loaded gun which he kept in his pocket. When Martha came out he took aim and shot her through the brain. She fell at his feet and he immediately turned the gun on himself but survived. The vicar of Wiveton was hanged at Tyburn just 50 days after his ordination.

The Reverend Harold Davidson, alias the Prostitutes' Padre, was vicar of Stiffkey, and defrocked in the 1930s. The press had a lot of fun with the double entendre attached to the name of his parish. Davidson loved London and his duties included being a chaplain for the Actors' Church Union. This kept him in the city for most of the week, but his local parishioners did not complain. They called him 'Little Jimmy', because he was so short, and lived with his eccentricities. It was said that it was best not to die on a Monday in hot weather, because he did not get back from London until late Saturday night!

The vicar soon earned himself an unfavourable reputation in town. He was banned from several theatres after being found in certain actresses' dressing rooms watching the costume changes. Many of his 'filles de joie' were brought back to the Norfolk vicarage for holidays, which caused ripples in the village and a stir with his hot-tempered Irish wife. He is said to have set up a dubious au pair agency for his London ladies and took them to France to live with local families.

Davidson ended up a bankrupt and a sideshow entertainer, doing bizarre acts. Invariably whenever he performed there was a sign beside him, protesting his innocence from the charges found against him in the ecclesiastical court. One of his stunts was being half roasted in an oven with a mechanical devil prodding him in his backside with a fork to see if he was done. The sad little man died soon after being half eaten by a lion who objected to 'the prostitutes' padre's' head being placed in his mouth. This was on 28th July 1937 in Captain Rye's Pavilion at the Skegness Amusement Park.

Two musicals were written about his flamboyant life, and both were flops. Harold Francis Davidson is buried in Stiffkey churchyard with his headstone facing the wrong way and its inscription erased by the weather. However 'Little Jimmy' is firmly fixed in Norfolk folklore.

WOLTERTON HALL

The White Lady

WOLTERTON HALL, which stands three and a half miles north-west of Blickling, is said to be haunted by 'The White Lady'. According to Lady Dorothy Neville, who wrote about her family in 'Mannington and the Walpoles', the spectre was in the habit of appearing just before there was a death or some trouble in the family. In 1894 her brother said to her, 'I hear from Norfolk that "The White Lady" has been seen again. It is you or I this time, Dolly, for we are the only ones left.' A few days later he was dead.

Lady Dorothy related a story that the phantom was one of the Scamler family who had owned Wolterton before the Walpoles. When the new hall was built some of the gravestones were unearthed from around the ruined church and the White Lady's resting place was disturbed. However, there had been no such act of vandalism, so there must be some other reason for the haunting. She said that in the olden days the Walpoles used to be driven in their hearse three times around this ruined church before being interred in the family vault.

WOODTON

Ned Baldry and his Horse

EDWARD (NED) BALDRY was born at Woodton, not far from the Suffolk border, in 1705. He had a horse which was to make him famous, and he only acquired it by chance.

At the age of 13 he was taken on by Squire Robert Suckling as a parish apprentice and employed as a stable boy at Woodton Hall. This used to stand behind All Saints church. The boy was soon promoted to kennel-keeper, then second 'whipper-in'. The squire had the finest pack of hounds for miles around, and from this post Baldry rose to become a celebrated huntsman.

His life changed on the day he went to Bungay Fair and bought a worn out old mare for a shilling or two. The bag of rattling bones was turned out into the orchard at the back of the hall. Her task was to eat herself to the boiling pot and feed the hounds. Two weeks later the squire examined the horse, and noticed the hint of a gleam in her eye and a sleekness about her coat. He decided to spare her. The following spring she produced a remarkably fine skewbald or 'shelled' colt, which was only to be ridden by Baldry. The horse and its master did well and their fame reached as far as Leicestershire, the prime hunting county of England.

One day a stranger called at Woodton and was taken to view the stables and kennels. Before leaving he threw down a challenge for the next day. It was to be horse and man! Leicestershire versus Norfolk! That morning the stable yard was bustling with anticipation. Every person connected with the hall, right down to the crow-boy, was unusually excited.

Both huntsmen set off to ride to the death if necessary. However, the contest ended in a draw. As the challenger prepared to go home, Ned insisted that he accompany him, at least for part of his journey. The fact that he mounted his 'shelled' horse, rather than a fresh one, hinted that he was determined to win the day. He would do it, even if he had to ride all the way to Leicestershire.

The two men got as far as Bungay, where The Tuns Inn was undergoing repairs. The sashes had been removed from the window frame of one of the rooms and the sill was about 4½ ft from the ground. Pointing his whip to the hole in the wall, Ned commanded his horse, 'Go it over! Come along, old boy!' and they ended up in the parlour. Before the astonished drinkers could wipe their mouths, Ned and his amazing mount were out again, having landed safely on the dangerously sloping pavement. Now it was the stranger's turn. He gave the command, but his horse would not budge and refused to be coaxed. Ned and the 'shell' had won victory for each other and their county.

Squire Suckling bequeathed his fine pack of hounds and the famous horse to his head huntsman, together with ample funds for their maintenance. The great sportsman went to Ireland where he and his mount received many honours. Later he visited France and hunted with the king at Versailles.

Ned Baldry died in 1759 and is buried in the parish church-yard. On his gravestone are the following lines:

> 'Here lies a Huntsman who was stout and bold,
> His judgement such as could not be controlled;
> Few of his calling with him compare

For skill in hunting fox or fallow deer;
He shewed his art in England, Ireland, France,
And rests in this churchyard, being his Last Chance.'

The 'shell' is buried in the park at Woodton Hall.

Strangely enough, in the wood along Nobb's Lane are the remains of another good hunter. This is April Shower, who was destroyed after an accident in 1910 and rests in a smartly railed-off plot.

WORSTEAD

A Devilish Wager

WHEN the Flemish weavers settled in East Anglia in the Middle Ages, they introduced a technique which produced a cloth of fine fibres and closely twisted yarn. Worstead, which lies some four miles south of North Walsham, became a centre for the manufacture of this material, which took its name from the village. Some of the weavers' houses still survive. They are large and lofty enough to take the 12 ft high weaving looms once used in this cottage industry. Each dwelling has a cellar in which to store the wool at a cool even temperature.

Sir Berney (Barney) Brograve of Worstead House and Waxham Hall also left his mark in this area. Walter Rye the Norfolk historian points out that 'nearly all the local instances of extreme cunning and audacity have been fathered on this man'. As already mentioned in the Waxham story, 'Owd Sir Barney' was claimed to have sold his soul to the Devil. According to this Worstead legend, he also made a wager with his Satanic Majesty, yet again offering his soul as payment!

It is said that one day Brograve made a reckless boast to his mowers that he could out-mow the Devil. Should he lose, the Devil could take his soul. 'Old Scratch' heard his idle boasting

109

and accepted the bet on the spot. A few days later Sir Berney thought better of it. He tried to cancel the agreement, without success.

Two acres of black-stalked beans were staked out side by side for the contest. However, as the fatal night drew close, the crafty squire had a word with the blacksmith. He had him make some small iron rods, about the height of the beanstalks, and stuck them firmly all over the Devil's acre.

At last it was time for the contest. The man made good progress on his land, mowing with great skill. However, his opponent had to keep stopping to mop his brow and sharpen his scythe on the whetstone. By now the baron was way ahead of his friend from Hell who called out, 'I say, Barney bor! Them bunks (thistles) do cut damned hard!'

It was not long before the devil gave up. Sir Berney Brograve's soul remained his own, at least for a while!

The White Lady

THE plain and spacious church of St Mary, started in 1379, is one of my favourites of all the magnificent Norfolk churches funded from the prosperous wool trade. At certain times in the summer you can see the St Mary's Guild of Spinners, Weavers and Dyers working at their looms which line the south wall.

A ghost story is centred around the 109 ft high tower. The church bells are always rung at midnight on the 24th December to welcome in Christmas Day. However, long ago it was claimed to be the time when the legendary 'White Lady' appeared. What she looked like and why she haunted is not known. However, it was a long established custom for people to visit the parish church on that occasion, not necessarily for worship, but in the hope of seeing the phantom.

In 1830 a man is claimed to have volunteered to climb into the belfry, bragging that if he saw the White Lady he would give her a kiss! It was a long climb up the ladder and the lofty tower remained eerily quiet. His friends called to him but he would not answer, so in the end they went up to fetch him. The no-longer daring man was found huddled in the ringing chamber, as if turned to stone. He was brought down and taken to the inn, where he was said to have regained enough life to whisper, 'I've seen her! I've seen her!' and then died.

People now go to church at midnight on Christmas Eve for the right reason, to celebrate Christ's Mass, and the White Lady keeps her distance. I use the present tense, as I am told that from time to time things which cannot be explained still happen in Worstead. The White Lady could still be active.

Apparently some 60 years ago the old vicarage doors used to open and close as if by an invisible hand. Even 30 years ago its occupants were having their bedclothes pulled from them.

However, the strangest tale was told to me by someone who claims first-hand knowledge. The incident occurred in the 1970s. It was a week after the Worstead Festival, so the month was August. This respected local man said that he was in the church and noticed a distressed looking woman praying by the font. Her husband got out his camera and took a photograph of her in prayer.

Sometime after Christmas a copy of the print was sent to a person connected with the church. It came with a note to say that it had only just been developed. My informant also saw it and recognised the woman whom he had seen in the summer. What was so amazing was that close behind her was the definite impression of a woman dressed in an ankle length smock. She was wearing a bonnet, with one stray curl laying against her cheek. The immediate reaction was that it was a hoax. A larger copy was taken, plus a slide negative which was projected onto a screen. It looked real enough.

Two years later, the gentleman who had witnessed the visitor at prayer in St Mary's, happened to be in the church when she called again. This time she looked very happy. He gave no hint that he had seen her before. The woman came up and explained that she was on a sort of pilgrimage. Two years before she had been very sick and troubled and had prayed for help by the font. God had answered her through the presence of a woman who had stood over her. She said that her husband had taken a photograph at that time and produced a copy as proof. She said that a print had been sent to the village and more conversation took place.

If this is genuine, I wonder if there is any connection between the figure standing behind the pilgrim and the White Lady? Either way, this could be a miraculous tale.

111

WYMONDHAM

Town versus Gown!

THE most splendid building in this market town between Norwich and Thetford is its abbey, where the nave has been preserved as the parish church. It has two towers; the west tower was started in about 1445 and the other, now ruined, was part of the monastery. The citizens of Wymondham (pronounced 'Windam') were constantly squabbling with the monks over who owned what in the church.

Wymondham Priory, which was raised to the status of an abbey just 90 years before its suppression, was founded in 1107 as a community of Benedictine monks. The founder, William D'Albini I, chief butler to Henry I, intended that the church should be used by both the priory and the townspeople as their parish church. No directions were given as to who should have which part. In time the priory pulled rank and the citizens of Wyndham resisted. Pope Innocent IV ruled in 1249 that the parishioners should have use, and not control, of the nave, north aisle and north-west tower. The priory should have the quire and eastern chapels, the transepts, the south aisle and the south-west tower.

More wrangling flared up when the original Norman tower was replaced by the octagonal design in 1376. Its new position made a rigid division between the monastic and parochial parts of the church. During building works the priory had placed its bells in the parishioners' north-west tower. However, when they were removed to the new tower, the monks blocked up the entrance to the other! The furious townspeople retaliated by destroying the barrier and hanging three bells of their own. They also filled in the monks' entrance to the nave, and imprisoned the prior in his south-west monastic tower for two days.

In 1411 Henry VI was asked to intervene. He ruled that the parishioners' bells could remain, so long as they were not rung at a time which would disturb the monks' meditation. It was not long before some 3,000 parishioners petitioned the monarch for permission to build a new and higher tower, so that their bells could be heard more clearly. Nothing was done until the middle of the 15th century when a large new building project was undertaken, which included a new west tower.

Not only did this priory disagree with the townspeople, it also fell out with its mother abbey at St Albans. Eventually Wymondham became an abbey in its own right. The Dissolution came 90 years later, when most of the building was pulled down. Fortunately the two towers remain plus the glorious church with its hammerbeam roof. You could say that the town won in the end!

William of the Strong Hand

AN interesting story surrounds the founder's son, William D'Albini II, who married the widow of Henry I. According to legend he was also known as 'William of the Strong Hand', and this is how he acquired the soubriquet.

The story says that the Queen of France, when a young and beautiful widow, fell in love with a gallant knight. She thought him the most wonderful man on earth. Therefore she ordered a tournament, promising to reward all the contestants according to their respective merits. Should there be an outstanding winner, and hopefully it would be her man, she would marry him without dishonour to herself. Brave warriors from all over the world hastened to Paris, including William d'Albini II. He fought magnificently and the queen immediately forgot her knight and fell in love with him. A splendid banquet was arranged in his honour and after giving him precious jewels, she proposed marriage.

However, he had already made wedding plans with the widowed Queen of England, so he refused the Queen of France. This angered her beyond measure and she made plans to be avenged. D'Albini was enticed into a secret cave which housed a hungry lion. When told of its fierceness, he laughed and said it was 'a womanish and not manly quality to be afraid'. Whereupon the queen opened a secret folding door and pushed him into the lion's den. He faced the great beast, removed his cloak and rolled it around his arm. Next he thrust his arm in the

113

animal's mouth, pulled its tongue out by the root and presented it to the Queen of France on a plate.

His fame returned with him to England, and he became known as 'William of the Strong Hand'. He was granted the Earldom of Arundel, 'and for his arms the lyon was given him'.

Glossary of Norfolk Dialect Words

Mostly gleaned from 'Broad Norfolk' contributed by readers of the *Eastern Daily Press* between the 21st January and the 19th March, 1949. All the words were either in current use or within memory.

Acculster	Axle
Allerwater	Thrashing
Ax	Ask
Backus	Wash-house
Bait the hoss	Feed the horse
Beaver	A snack eaten at 11 am
Bishy Barnabees	Ladybirds
Blaa	Cry, as in 'He ball-ed and blaa-ed'
Black as the Hakes	Usually applied to children's hands being as black and dirty as the hakes or hooks in the chimney from which cooking pots were hung
Blackmeat	Bacon
Black-stalk	Chimney
Blee	To resemble, 'You do blee your father!'
Bop	Stoop
Bor	A boy or youth
Brief	A letter
Bulk	A throbbing wound
Buskins	Leather leggings
Caanser	Causeway
Caddow	Jackdaw
Canker	Caterpillar
Carny	To wheedle
Chelp	Cheek, 'I want none of your chelp!'

115

Chicked	When seeds have burst; children would watch carefully to see when their mustard and cress grown on damp cotton wool had chicked
Chin music	Crying
Clarty	Sticky, a sugary mess
Clawth	Pain
Clung	Juiceless, withered or wilted
Cobbles	Fruit stones
Colder	Broken straw and refuse after threshing
Cooshies	Sweets
Cowt breearking	Breaking in a colt
Crowd	Push, 'To crowd the cooch' – push the pram
Cruckle	Crust
Cyprus cat	A tabby or brindled cat
Daggly	Damp, usually used with reference to the weather, 'A daggly ol' day'
Dannicks	Sparrows
Dannocks	Mittens, hedging gloves
Dannys	Children's hands
Dawzle	To daze
Deke	Dyke or bank
Dickey	Donkey
Ding	A blow, 'A ding on yer lug' – blow on your ear
Dissables	Shabby clothes
Dodmans	Snails
Draw	To walk or wander, 'Well, I best be a-drawin' on!'
Dumpling hunter	Local preacher
Dutfin/dutphin	Horse's bridle
Du	Do
Duller	Noise, as in 'Hold your duller' – stop making a noise
Dum-ducker-du-mur	A mixture of colours
Dwandly/dwainy	Weak, 'Them cabbages is kinda dwandly'

116

Dwile/dwoile	Floor cloth; also used as a term of disapprobation for a lady – 'You mucky ol' dwile you!'
Dydle	To bail out, dredge
Fall	A veil
Fare as if	It seems that
Fintums	Fuss over food
Firlpen	Dustpan
Flag-fire	Bonfire
Foosey	Withered, 'A foosey turnip'
Frame	To put on airs, 'Look at her framing about!'
Froise	A poor person's pancake
Funny	Extremely, 'That's a funny good hoss!'
Fye out	Clean out (a ditch etc)
Gallusdroply	Foul-mouthed, evil-looking
Gammarattle	'Thas all gammarattle' – nonsense, rubbish
Gant	Village fair
Garn	Give
Garping	Staring
Gays	Scraps pasted in a scrapbook, 'Reading the gays' – looking through the scrapbook
Gimbling	Sniggering
Go cart	Wicker-work perambulator on three wheels
Gostlings	Willow buds
Gowsbra	Gooseberry
Grane	Strangle
Gripple	A small ditch or trench to drain off surface water
Grunkle	A pain, 'My shoulder grunkles'
Grunny	Gutter
Grup	See 'Gripple'
Guler	A mischievous child

Hah and hacker	Stammer
Hain	Raise, in connection with wages
Hazed	Washing when partly dry
Highlows	Boots with tops which reached just above the ankles
High sprites	Ghosts or goblins
High-strikers	Hysterics
Hinderpart	The back of anything
Hocking	Tripping or kicking an opponent in football
Hod-me-dods	Snails
Holdjer	The small boy riding a horse pulling a wagon being loaded with sheaves would·call 'Holdjer!' to the loader before moving – meaning 'Hold yourself' or 'Hold fast' – he was usually known as the 'Holdjer Boy'
Holl	Ditch
Hollow meat	Rabbit meat
Horfling	Walking or moving awkwardly
Hoss	Horse
Hoss it up	Lift it up
Howsomever	However
Huckering	To keep going on about something
Hulls	Pods
Hulver	Holly
Hummer	A lie
Hutkin	Finger stall
Huxterer	Dealer in rabbit skins and odds and ends
Imitate	Attempt
Jiffling	Fidgeting
Jimmers	A hinge
Jumpin' Jacks	Frogs
Kail	Lift up
Killer	A small tub
King Harry	A goldfish

118

Kiser	Cheese
Kit	A milk can
Koished	Thrashed
Kyish	Smug or shy, 'Looking kyish'
Lampering	Striding, loping, 'A regular lamperer' – a fast walker
Lantern jaw'd	Someone who is always complaining about their health
Lickup	Small quantity – a dollop
Ligger	A single plank bridge
'Lijahs	Straps worn over the trouser legs just below the knees
Loke	Lane
Lumberin'	A noise
Malted	Hot and bothered
Mantle	A coarse apron for rough work
Mardle	To gossip
Masterpiece	Something extraordinary
Mawkin	Scarecrow
Mawther	Girl
Mellow	Ripe, 'Are your pears mellow?'
Million	A large pumpkin or marrow
Mingins	Gnats
Mivey	Mouth
Moise	A bullock is moising when he is fattening well
Moithered	Worried
Muckwash	Hot and bothered, sweaty
My little man/woman	Term of endearment for tiny baby, or boy or girl
Nasty particular	Fussy
Neat'us/neathouse	Cowshed or milking shed
Nijjerten	Attending a woman in labour
Nointer	A rascal
Nonicking	Horseplay
One journey	Working without a meal break

Pah yard	Muck yard
Paigle	Cowslip
Pamplin	Walking carefully
Passe	Badly upset or annoyed
Ped	Wicker basket with lid
Peerking	Nosing around
Pensy	To be off colour, feeling unwell
Perk	Perch
Piece	Field
Pightle	Small field
Pike off!	Go away
Pingle	To toy with one's food
Pinpaches	Winkles
Pishmares/pissamare	An ant
Pissamare-Barnabee	An earwig
Plawks	Hands
Plump	Bread soaked in hot water to which butter, sugar or dripping has been added
Poddle-ladle	A tadpole
Poke	A small bag, hence the saying 'A pig in a poke'
Popple	Nonsense
Porking/pawking	Gathering firewood, especially driftwood from the beach
Pricker bag	Dinner bag
Primicky	Hard to please
Prugging about	Wandering about
Puckaterry	Hot and bothered
Pug	'I'll jest pug these through!' – to wash a few clothes quickly and not thoroughly
Puke	A disagreeable person
Pulk	A small pit of stagnant water
Push	A boil
Quackle	Choke
Quarter arter	Quarter past the hour, 'Two or three minutes arter quarter arter' –

	two or three minutes after quarter past
Quicks	Corn stubble
Rafty	Stale or fusty, or misty weather
Rare thacking	A good beating
Reel-a-bobbin	Cotton reel
Ride the grey mare	Rule your husband
Roke	Fog or mist, 'Rokey day'
Rorping	An animal which is making a troublesome noise, often used of a bull
Rume o'	In room of, instead of
Run	Leak – Norfolk kettles don't leak, they run!
Runnel	Wheel
Sawney/suke	Foolish person, a half-witted country bumpkin
Scrog	To cut beans with a reaphook
Scutes	Odd bits and corners of an otherwise well-shaped field
Seal/sel/sele	Time, season, 'Keeps bad seals' – keeps bad hours, 'I just give him the seal of day' – to nod at someone and pass them by Haysel – time of haymaking Barksel – time of stripping bark from trees Barleysel – time of sowing barley (word thought to be of Saxon origin)
Serstificate	A certificate
Shail	Throw up
Shanny	Over excited, crazy
Shiver	A wood splinter
Shucky	Untidy, dishevelled
Shug	To shake

Shywanikan	Boisterous and suggesting a lot of movement – often used to describe frightened hens
Sibits	Marriage banns
Slarver	Talk (used contemptuously)
Sluggish	Strongly built
Smittick	A tiny piece
Smur	Drizzle, 'It's smurring'
Snack	A door latch
Snearth	Candle wick
Sneerfroys	Supercilious
Sosh	Slanting 'On the sosh' – it slants down
Soshins	Crosswise, 'Put it soshins' – neatly across
Sow	Woodlouse
Spantry	Threshold
Splaar	Spread
Spolt	Short grained (rhymes with 'bolt') (When a haymaker broke his fork shaft, he excused himself by saying, 'Y'see, master, that owd bit o' ash is werry spolt' The word can also indicate crispness, 'Them radishes is nice and spolt'
Sprung	Cracked or split
Stewping	Drinking noisily
Stive	Dust, 'To kick up a stive' – to stir up dust
Stupid upright	Just off the vertical
Sunket	A little
Suslams	A mixture of foods such as trifle
Swale	Shade
Swaliking	Sweltering
Swar'ston winder	A smack in the face
Swimmer	A dumpling – often known as '20 minute swimmers' because that is how long it takes to boil them

Tempest	Thunderstorm
Things are up at arridge (Harwich)	Things are in a muddle
Tie	A pinafore
Tittermatorter	See-saw
Tizzack	A persistent or rasping cough
Tom and Jerry	Any public house of ill repute
Tom Mogg	A tom cat
Tom Noddy	A tadpole
Tricolate	Tidy up, put into a good state of repair
Twiltin	A good thrashing
Uvly	Sulky
Vacagees	Wartime evacuees
Werry	Very, 'Werry werry bad!'
Wetshed	Wet feet, possibly 'wet shod'
Whelm	To upturn a pail after use
Wibbled	Untidily packed
Widder/widdles	Whitlows
Widdles	Pimples
Winnicking	Whimpering
Wittles	Food
Wittery	Weak, 'A raly wittery woman' – a really weak woman
Yalm	To eat

Bibliography

The Saving of Sarah Hare Pamphlet written by Monica Dance
The Folklore of East Anglia Enid Porter, B T Batsford Ltd, London
The History & Legends of the Broad District Ernest E Suffling, Jarrold & Sons
East Anglia Curiosities Rick O'Brien, The Dovecote Press
Ghosts & Witches J Wentworth Day, B T Batsford
Norfolk Notes & Queries
Highways & Byways in East Anglia William A Dutt, MacMillan & Co
The Norfolk Village Book Compiled by the Norfolk Federation of Women's Institutes, Countryside Books, Newbury and NFWI Norfolk
Walstan of Bawburgh Edited by Carol Twinch, Media Associates, Norwich
Gothick Norfolk Jennifer Westwood, Shire Publications
The Norfolk Garland John Glyde Jun, Jarrold & Sons
A Norfolk Anthology Caroline Fendall, The Boydell Press, Ipswich
True Ghost Stories Marchioness Townshend of Raynham and I M C Ffoulkes
Ballads, Songs and Rhymes of East Anglia A S Harvey, Jarrold & Sons Ltd
The Maddermarket Theatre Hilda Wells
Hidden Norfolk F V Morley, Methuen & Co Ltd
In Breckland Wilds R Rainbird Clark, W Heffer & Sons Ltd
The Companion Guide to East Anglia John Seymour, Collins
East Anglian Ghosts, Legends & Lore Peter Jeffrey, The Old Orchard Press
The Norfolk Guide Wilhelmine Harrod, The Alastair Press
The Mayor of Casterbridge Thomas Hardy, Penguin Classics
Broad Norfolk Jonathan Mardle, Wensum Books
A Short History of the English People John Richard Green, MacMillan & Co Ltd
The Oxford History of Britain Edited by Kenneth O Morgan, Oxford University Press
Wymondham Abbey Printed by Miro Press, Bury St Edmunds
The Book of Margery Kempe 1436 W Butler-Bowdon, Jonathan Cape 1936

Acknowledgements

Special thanks to the Folklore Society for permission to use their archive material collected by the late Miss Matthews of Watford. Also to the editor of the *Eastern Daily Press* for his kind permission to use material from the 'Broad Norfolk' articles published between January and March, 1949.

I am also grateful to the following for their generous help: Norfolk Libraries and Information Service; The Construction Industry Training Board, Bircham Newton; The White Lion Hotel, Holt; Mr David Govan and Mrs Terry Carter from The Bell, Thetford; Mr Fred Gurney; the staff of the Ancient House Museum, Thetford; Mr David Harris, Artistic Director, Maddermarket Theatre, Norwich; Mr Chris Lucas, Head Custodian, Grimes Graves; The King's Lynn Tourist Information Centre; Mr T Mouse; Ms Sarah Magroo; Mr Pat Palmer, manager of The Hare Arms, Stow Bardolph; Mr Joe Wright; Mrs Anita Perks; Mr Alan Taylor; Mr and Mrs R Phoenix; Mr H Raven; Mr Andrew Kedar; Mr Bill Brownlow; and my husband Duncan Howat.

Index